Few people have done more to shine a [...] Bible than Steve Green. His passion, vision, and sheer tenacity for exposing the magnificence of Scripture have reshaped American culture and given future generations a firm foundation on which to build their faith.

DAVID AND JASON BENHAM, AUTHORS,
SPEAKERS, ENTREPRENEURS

Steve loves the Bible. In his new work, he helps us to gain an even greater appreciation for what God says in his written message to us, the Bible. I highly recommend *This Beautiful Book* to you.

GREG LAURIE, PASTOR, HARVEST CHURCH;
EVANGELIST, HARVEST CRUSADES

Steve has once again produced a work that illuminates the Bible. *This Beautiful Book* provides the narrative of the Bible to its readers in a thoughtful, digestible way.

CARLY FIORINA, FOUNDER, CARLY
FIORINA ENTERPRISES

In spite of the fact that biblical stories may be offensive to the sensibilities of many in our increasingly thin-skinned culture, Steve helps us understand why and how the Bible remains relevant and even transformational for so many.

BYRON R. JOHNSON, PROFESSOR,
BAYLOR UNIVERSITY

Steve uses small words to tell a big story—my kind of read—clarity for a first-rate cause.

JERRY PATTENGALE, AUTHOR, *IS THE BIBLE AT FAULT?*

Helpful. Inspiring. A great tool to help us grow in our understanding of God's Word. Steve helps us realize that Scripture tells one overarching story, centered on the work and person of Jesus, and helps us to see how good God is and how great his love is for us.

LOUIE GIGLIO, PASTOR, PASSION CITY
CHURCH; AUTHOR, NOT FORSAKEN

Here's a majestic and personal tour of the most influential book in history—a creative and comprehensive guide to unlocking the Bible's magnificent story of redemption and hope. Highly recommended!

LEE STROBEL, AUTHOR, THE CASE FOR
CHRIST AND THE CASE FOR FAITH

Steve introduces the reader to the "big story" of the Bible and shows his passion for helping readers who are unfamiliar with the Good Book. Bravo!

ERIC METAXAS, AUTHOR; HOST, ERIC
METAXAS RADIO SHOW

This is the tremendous contribution of Steve and Bill in *This Beautiful Book*: they take seriously biblical scholarship but effectively provide the reader with a larger narrative, an understandable introduction, and a sincere call to engage the beautiful story of the Bible.

L. RANDOLPH LOWRY, PRESIDENT, LIPSCOMB UNIVERSITY

THIS
BEAUTIFUL
BOOK

THIS
BEAUTIFUL
BOOK

AN EXPLORATION OF THE BIBLE'S INCREDIBLE
STORY LINE AND WHY IT MATTERS TODAY

STEVE GREEN

with BILL HIGH

ZONDERVAN BOOKS

This Beautiful Book
Copyright © 2019 by Steve Green and William High

Published in Grand Rapids, Michigan, by Zondervan. Zondervan is a registered
trademark of The Zondervan Corporation, L.L.C., a wholly owned subsidiary of
HarperCollins Christian Publishing, Inc.

Requests for information should be addressed to customercare@harpercollins.com.

Zondervan titles may be purchased in bulk for educational, business, fundraising, or
sales promotional use. For information, please email SpecialMarkets@Zondervan.com.

ISBN 978-0-310-35602-8 (hardcover)
ISBN 978-0-310-36929-5 (softcover)
ISBN 978-0-310-35613-4 (audio)
ISBN 978-0-310-35611-0 (ebook)

Author is represented by the Christopher Ferebee Agency, www.christopherferebee.com.

Cover design: James W. Hall IV
Cover illustration: © aleabievsasha / Depositphotos
Interior design: Emily Ghattas

$PrintCode

To my six children, their spouses, and their children, and all who are yet to come. There is nothing more I would like to leave you than the story this book summarizes.

CONTENTS

CONTENTS

INTRODUCTION

KNOWING THE STORY

What's your favorite movie or play? For some people, it might be *Star Wars* or something classic like *It's a Wonderful Life*. If it's a Broadway musical, I suspect some might think of *Les Misérables*. Except for me—at least at first.

I used to travel to NYC once a year on a business trip. When it was possible for my wife, Jackie, to join me, we'd do our best to attend a Broadway play. One year, we decided to see *Les Misérables*, a story set during a time of rebellion in France when the common man was fighting for what was right. I had heard about the story and understood it to be a good one. Some of our friends said it was one of their favorites. I didn't know the story but decided to go anyway.

At the intermission of the play, I was confused.

"What were the names of the main characters again?" I asked my wife. Not only did I have trouble remembering the characters' names, but I couldn't tell who was who.

It was a musical, and I admit I have never been accused of being highly cultured, but I was having a hard time following the story line. There was this guy named Jean Valjean and another guy named Javert, and I couldn't distinguish between the two, especially when they were singing their names.

During the intermission, we noticed a bit of the story line that was given in the playbill. That was helpful. Jackie and I were still trying to read the plotline when the lights went off for the second act.

After we left the theater, I felt disappointed with the evening. I didn't have a clue to what I had just seen.

Not wanting to give up on the story, I decided to watch the movie. I was not going to try the book, as that would be too much of a commitment, especially if I wound up not liking the story. After watching the movie for an hour and a half, I discovered that I loved the story. Now that I knew the story, I wondered if I would enjoy the Broadway play.

On our next trip to NYC, Jackie and I once again attended *Les Misérables*, and what do you know—I was able to follow the story line, and I loved it. It is one of my all-time favorite Broadway plays. We've returned several times to see it.

Now when friends ask me for a Broadway musical recommendation, I always suggest *Les Misérables* if it's playing. I also suggest they at least watch one of the movie versions if they're not familiar with the story, because it made a world of difference for me.

THE STORY I SEE

The primary purpose for me in writing this book is to explain as best I can the story of the Bible from my perspective so that it makes a little more sense as you read it. Let me explain what I mean when I say, "from my perspective."

Imagine you and three of your friends go see a movie one Friday night. After the movie, you head to your favorite diner, and as you sit drinking coffee or eating late-night pancakes, you each explain the story of the movie.

Each person would cover their unique view of the story—their perspective of it. The plot is the same—the good guy, the bad guy, the problem and resolution all the same—but each of you highlights different parts of the story. Each points out parts that they found interesting, but the story doesn't change. Now imagine that's what you and I are doing right now. This book is our diner, our meeting place, and you and I are sitting at a table, and I'm attempting to explain the story of the Bible from my perspective. The story could be told in a variety of ways, but it would remain the same. This just happens to be the way I choose to tell the story.

My secondary purpose is to show how the many stories of the Bible come together to tell a single story. I've learned to see the Bible as a unified story. Imagine me as your tour guide. I'll let the Bible speak for itself as much as I can, and I'll fill in the gaps as we go, pointing out some interesting things and moving on. My hope is, you will want to explore for yourself to see if I've got it right.

SEEING THE BIG PICTURE

Recently, I was in an Australian-themed restaurant with my youngest daughter. On the wall there was a picture of Uluru, or what is called Ayers Rock, which is located in central Australia. From a distance, it was easy to see the picture of the popular destination, but when you got closer, you noticed the picture was made up of many smaller pictures. When you looked closely at the smaller pictures, the bigger picture was indiscernible. The smaller pictures were interesting, but what made the whole thing especially interesting was how, when put together, the smaller pictures made the bigger picture.

This is how I see the Bible and what I am trying to

do with this book. I want to step back with you and see the larger picture that all the smaller stories of the Bible, when put together, make up. What I hope you will see is that the Bible is a beautiful book made up of many stories and that those stories connect themselves to tell a larger story—a beautiful story.

ONE

THE BIG PICTURE

This beautiful story begins with a God who creates all things, including the human race, and declares everything that he made good. A problem arises in the story when human beings disobey God. Their disobedience results in separation in their relationship with the creator God. How will they ever be reconnected with their Creator?

Spoiler alert! God, then, sends his Son, Jesus, to pay the price for the broken relationship and offers restoration to any who accept.

Now that I just told you the story, you don't even need

to read this book. You can go straight to the Bible and read it for yourself. But if you want to have a little more of the story fleshed out, then keep on reading.

KNOWING THE STORY HELPS

Today our knowledge of the Bible continues to decline. Some people know very little about the Bible. Not long ago, I attended a meeting in NYC, and a journalist from one of the major news outlets said that he had colleagues in his office who did not know what the Easter holiday was about.

It's understandable that we know less about the Bible today, since we don't teach it as we once did. The Bible used to be taught in public schools, but the *Engel v. Vitale* Supreme Court ruling in 1962 began the eventual removal of Bible teaching in school.[1]

That is part of the motivation for this book. I think it is good to have a basic understanding of the story of the Bible. But the Bible is a big book and can be very confusing at times.

Maybe you have heard some of the Bible's stories but haven't read the entire book and, like me during intermission at *Les Misérables*, you don't know how the stories connect or if they connect at all. Or maybe you don't know any of the Bible's stories and feel left out when someone at work brings up the current holiday, which happens to be connected to the story of the Bible.

Wherever you are in your Bible reading journey, this book represents my effort to provide a basic understanding of the Bible's story.

Simple enough, right?

Not really. The problem is, the Bible is controversial. I realize that you can't create anything concerning the Bible without someone criticizing what you did or how you did it. I can already hear the objections.

"Well, that is your version of the Bible."

Or, "What Bible are you talking about? Don't you know there are several Bibles?"

Or, "Don't you know that the Bible is made up?"

Or maybe this one: "The Bible is just a collection of stories that doesn't tell a single story."

Yes, I understand that no matter how I tell the Bible's story, naysayers will naysay. And that's okay. That will never change.

From my experience, I've found that the best way to understand what the Bible is about is to read it for yourself. And I hope you do.

BUT THE CONTROVERSIES . . .

The Bible I grew up reading had sixty-six books, divided into thirty-nine Old Testament books and twenty-seven New Testament books.

I see two main differences with other versions of the

Bible. The Bible in the Jewish tradition includes only the Old Testament, though they do not call it that—rather, simply the Bible. Though there is a different sequence of books and different divisions of the text, the content of the books in the Jewish Bible is virtually identical to what I call the Old Testament. The basic characters and stories are the same. Throughout this book, I will use the terms Old and New Testament.

The other difference deals with the Apocrypha. This is a group of relatively short books considered to be part of the Bible by some faith traditions, like Catholicism. For groups that include the Apocrypha, the number varies. But the Bible of my youth has no Apocrypha.

As I tell the Bible's story, there are many of the sixty-six books I grew up with that I do not cover. So even if you do include the Apocrypha as part of your Bible, the story that I am telling doesn't change. For the Jewish reader, my ending is much different, which leads to understanding the Jewish Bible differently. Maybe you don't agree with the ending of the story I tell. I ask that you humor me, if you will. Let me tell the ending as told by the New Testament. You can decide what you do with it.

Some make a big deal about the differences. But beyond the two main ones I've just described, the differences are minor and do not affect the subjects or theses of the Bible.

The preceding discussion of Bible versions does not

include different translations of the Bible. The King James Version (KJV), the New International Version (NIV), and the English Standard Version (ESV) are three of the many English translations of the Bible. Unless you are reading the Bible in the original languages of Hebrew in the Old Testament or primarily Greek in the New Testament, you are reading a translation.

There are thousands of translations of the Bible in hundreds of languages. Some people argue over which translation is best or most accurate or easiest to read. My purpose is not to delve into these arguments. When I quote from the Bible, I will be using the New International Version (NIV) unless noted otherwise. My suggestion? Pick one and read it.

Another point of contention is the truth, or lack thereof, of the Bible. There are millions of people who believe the Bible to be true, and millions who don't. Both sides can become very passionate about their beliefs. And both sides have published many books about their view of the Bible's veracity. The purpose of this book, however, is not to address or have an in-depth discussion on whether the Bible is true; it is simply to tell the story.

The books of the Bible I grew up with were divided into chapters and verses. This is common today and is embraced by many faith traditions, but those divisions were not part of the original writings. They are very useful as a way of directing a person's attention to a particular spot in the Bible. I will use those markers throughout this book. If you're brand-new to the Bible, I recommend familiarizing yourself with the books of the Bible, because I will be making references to them regularly in this book. You can find a list in the appendix at the end of this book.

While we could spend the rest of this book addressing the controversies associated with the Bible, I will leave it at that because talking about the controversies is not the purpose of this book either.

For some of you, this book may be your introduction to the Bible. You may be starting from scratch. I think that's fantastic. For others who might possess some knowledge of the Bible, I'd like to suggest setting aside whatever you do know about it and embracing this opportunity to look at the Bible with new eyes.

KEEPING THINGS IN ORDER

One more thing before we get into the story.

As in many stories, there's a timeline in the story of the Bible. I will refer to it as the biblical timeline—another topic for controversy that we won't get into. However, I find it helpful to keep things in order, so I understand how the stories fit together. Let's start with a big timeline to which we can refer throughout our journey. The story begins with the beginning and ends with the end. What a novel idea.

The story starts with the creation of the world and everything in it. I won't put a date on creation, but we can look at five of the main characters in the Bible and give an approximate date for their lives within the Bible's story. And remember, when looking at the historical timeline, dates in the BC era count down, unlike those in the AD era, which count up.

The first main character is Abraham. The story introduces him early. We can place Abraham's life at around 2000 BC.

Next is Moses. The Bible credits the first five books of the Bible to Moses. He comes in around five hundred years after Abraham, which puts him somewhere near 1500 BC.

Coming in around 1000 BC is King David, a well-known figure in the Bible.

The next character I will pick is Isaiah. The Bible places him around 700 BC.

These four figures are written about in the Old Testament. The last figure is the main character in the New Testament. His name is Jesus. Our calendar is tied to his birth. Let's place him at AD 1.

The world history timeline begins counting up after the birth of Jesus. We live in the twenty-first century, two thousand years since the birth of Jesus. For centuries, the world has used the labels AD and BC to mark the major eras of world history. In today's modern era, the Gregorian calendar is used by the world as a standard by which we keep track of years.

The label AD stands for *anno Domini*, which is a Latin term meaning "in the year of the Lord." You may recall hearing people in official business of the state or federal governments use the phrase "in the year of our Lord." The modern world uses this label when referring to calendar dates after the birth of Jesus of Nazareth.

The label BC stands for "before Christ," referring to the era before the birth of Jesus. Though many countries and institutions do not ascribe to the religious foundations of the calendar system, nearly all agree to use it in the spirit of universal practicality. Interestingly, *The Oxford Companion to the Year* states, "If it is not an era of the Incarnation it is an era of nothing at all, for there is no known event in either 1 BC or AD 1 deserving of universal commemoration."[2] When they mention the incarnation, they are making reference to Jesus' birth.

The story doesn't end with Jesus. However, much of the New Testament is focused on his life. It ends looking into the future, which goes on for eternity. This, again, is a good topic for an argument.

So from time to time, I will come back to these characters as a way to get our bearings. Keep this in mind and refer back to the following chart as needed.

Creation	
Abraham	2000 BC
Moses	1500 BC
David	1000 BC
Isaiah	700 BC
Jesus	AD 1
Eternity	

Let's dive in. To begin our journey, I want to tell one of the stories of the Bible that you probably have not heard—the story of Mephibosheth. It's about a little picture within a big picture.

TWO

MEPHIBOSHETH: THE STORY WITHIN THE STORY

When I was newly married, Tom, the youth pastor of the small church I grew up in, asked me if I would teach a class for young married couples. I remember thinking, *I don't teach. I'm an introvert. I don't know the Bible enough to teach it to others.* On and on my excuses went. But Tom was a persistent encourager, and I relented.

Later, Tom came up with a new way for me to teach. He recommended I teach the Bible from beginning to end, going through seven chapters a week. In less than three and a half years, you could go through the whole Bible.

Again I was hesitant.

In the past, I had taught from study material I was provided. Tom's approach would mean that I would be on my own. Tom suggested we meet once a week over lunch so that he could help me with the lesson.

So off we went. And in around three and a half years, we'd traveled through the entire Bible. I still have some of those lessons.

Teaching through the Bible created a desire in me to keep the routine going. Only, now I'm reading through it on a regular basis. I will often start a new year with a reading plan that takes me through the Bible in a year. I have used a chronological Bible plan, in which there is an effort to put the stories in order of the biblical timeline. Another popular way to read the Bible in a year is to read a part of the Old Testament and a part of the New Testament every day so that the "slower" parts are broken up. There are many different Bible-in-a-year plans, and I have used several. When I read through the Bible in a year, I read several chapters every day without slowing down to investigate the details of my reading.

From time to time, I still teach a class at church, which is a much different experience than my yearly reading. But I have learned from both experiences. When I teach a class, I spend a lot of time on a small section of the Bible, digging in to learn what I can from that section. I may refer to my Bible program on my computer, which has many commentaries and study aids, or listen to sermons from others who have spent hours studying the passage and years in seminary studying the Bible.

I'm floored by how much I learn in the process of digging, and even more impressed with how much I learn from teaching.

Okay, enough about teaching in general. One Sunday, I taught on a very specific story, the story of Mephibosheth. That's right, that's a real name: Mephibosheth.

The story of Mephibosheth is easy to miss. And of course, you tend to skip over those hard Bible names anyway. By the way, it's pronounced Muh-FIB-o-sheth.

The first mention of Mephibosheth could be described as a parenthetical comment. King Saul reigned in the nation of Israel, but after he and his son Jonathan die in battle, a power struggle ensues. A shepherd boy named David (yes, the David from our timeline) is appointed king over Judah, while King Saul's son Ish-Bosheth (I know, another hard name) is appointed king over the remaining eleven tribes, or family units, of Israel. There is a long war between the rivals, and in the middle of this narrative, there's this curious insertion that feels out of place. We are told in 2 Samuel 4:4, "Jonathan son of Saul had a son who was lame in both feet. He was five years old when the news about Saul and Jonathan came from Jezreel. His nurse picked him up and fled, but as she hurried to leave, he fell and became disabled. His name was Mephibosheth."

That's it. Four sentences. It really doesn't make sense, standing alone. What we are told is that Jonathan, the son of Saul, had a son—Mephibosheth, a five-year-old boy. After Saul and Jonathan died, Mephibosheth's nurse picked him up to flee. An accident happened. Did he have to jump out a window? Did the nurse fall on him? We aren't told; we know only that Mephibosheth became lame.

Then the narrative of 2 Samuel 4 returns to the main story—the war between David and Ish-Bosheth. Ultimately, Ish-Bosheth is assassinated, and the kingdom of Israel is united under David's rule.

I know this piece of information about Jonathan's son is unnecessary if you read 2 Samuel 4 by itself. At best, you might wonder why Mephibosheth matters. Most of us would probably ignore it as irrelevant. That's what I do with this kind of information when I read the Bible in a year.

But let's pause for a moment and take a closer look. Who is David? Who is Saul? And how does Mephibosheth fit into the story? That's what I had to do when Mephibosheth became the topic of a lesson I was to teach.

DAVID, SAUL, AND MEPHIBOSHETH

King Saul was the first king of Israel. And even though the nation of Israel had high hopes that having a king would bring them deliverance from the oppression they were experiencing, Saul proves to be a flawed king. Instead of obeying God, he takes matters into his own hands to act as his own priest. As a result, God decides to replace him as king. Saul is told, "The LORD has sought out a man after his own heart and appointed him ruler of his people, because you have not kept the LORD's command" (1 Sam. 13:14).

That man after God's own heart proves to be David. He is described as "the LORD's anointed" (1 Sam. 16:6).

David's beginnings were humble. He was the youngest of eight sons. When his older brothers were summoned to war, David was left to take care of the sheep. He also served as messenger. His dad asked him to take supplies for his older brothers to the front lines of battle. Once he arrived, he found a standoff between the two armies.

You may recall this story.

The opposing army sent out their champion, a giant of a man named Goliath, who stood more than nine feet tall. He challenged the nation of Israel to send their champion out, so they could settle things mano a mano.

When David heard Goliath mouthing off to the army of Israel, he was enraged and volunteered to go teach the giant a lesson. His brothers mocked him and told him to shut up. And when he stood before King Saul, the king couldn't believe his eyes.

"You want to face this crazy giant? Well, okay, but wear my armor so you at least stand a chance." That's my paraphrase.

So the king sent him out, and David surprised everyone by killing the giant, without the king's armor!

You may recall the famous seventeen-foot statue of David by Michelangelo. Today it stands in the Gallery of the Academy museum in Florence, Italy. Michelangelo was twenty-six years old when he started the carving, and between 1501 and 1504, he worked to create one of the most well-known sculptures of all time. With a sling over his left shoulder and three stones hidden inside his right hand, David is depicted just as he is about to slay Goliath.

Now, I've skimmed over one of the best-known and most beloved stories in the Bible—a story that's embedded in popular culture—in order to give you a little background on David. After he killed the giant, the people of Israel loved him, and after the disobedience and the fall of Saul, he eventually ascended to be king of Israel.

All of that takes us back to 2 Samuel 4, where we have this seemingly out-of-place parenthetical statement about five-year-old, crippled Mephibosheth. As I said, that's the only mention of him at that place in the Bible. After that interlude, David's rise continues. He conquers Jerusalem, defeats his archenemies the Philistines, brings the ark of the covenant—a sacred item for the Jewish people—to Jerusalem, begins making plans to build a temple, and has a series of military victories to secure his throne.

Whew!

With his kingdom firmly established, David now has

time to pause and reflect on the past, and on his friendship with Jonathan, Saul's son. That's when Mephibosheth enters the story again.

A PROMISE MADE, A PROMISE KEPT

In the Old Testament book of 2 Samuel, chapter 9 begins with David asking a question. And his question drops a clue as to the theme of this little story.

"Is there anyone left of Saul's family? If so, I'd like to show him some kindness in honor of Jonathan."

One of Saul's top servants, Ziba, answers King David.

"Yes, there is Jonathan's son, Mephibosheth. He is lame in both feet."

"Where is he?" David asks.

"He's living at the home of Makir son of Ammiel in Lo Debar," Ziba replies.

The implication of Lo Debar is that it is a faraway place, in the wilderness, off the beaten path. It is a place to hide away.

David feels a sense of joy because Jonathan, the son of Saul, was one of his best friends. And one of the last things the two friends discussed was the future of Jonathan's family. David promised his friend that he would care for his family and show them favor in the future if Jonathan were to die. In finding that Mephibosheth is the son of Jonathan, David realizes he can fulfill his promise to his best friend.

So David sends for Mephibosheth. When Mephibosheth arrives and sees David, he bows as an act of honor to the king.

"Mephibosheth!" says David.

"Yes?" replies Mephibosheth.

"Don't be frightened," says David. "I'd like to do something special for you in memory of your father, Jonathan. To begin with, I'm returning to you all the properties of your grandfather, Saul. Furthermore, from now on you'll take all your meals at my table."

Mephibosheth can't believe his ears. He can't believe David would show such kindness to him. But why does he feel this way? Well, we have to know the whole story. Let's turn the pages back, for a moment, on the tenuous relationship between David and Saul.

Though David and Jonathan were best friends, David and Jonathan's father, King Saul, were not. At one point, when David was a young man serving in King Saul's court, playing music for him to help soothe his mind, Saul tried to kill him.

But eventually David fled Saul's court and became an outlaw. He lived in the wilderness with other outlaws and amassed quite a following of vagabonds. Once, when Saul was chasing David in the wilderness, David had the opportunity to kill him but didn't take it. David and his men were hiding out in caves. Saul walked into the very cave David and his men were hiding in, so that he could use the bathroom.

David's men urged him to kill Saul and end their days as vagabonds, but David would not touch Saul, because he knew that even though Saul was doing the wrong thing in chasing David, Saul was still God's anointed king of Israel. So David cut off the hem of Saul's robe while Saul was relieving himself and followed him out of the cave. Once Saul was far enough away from David, David shouted to him and held up the fabric of his robe, revealing to Saul that he had showed him mercy.

So Saul and David were not chummy. Quite the opposite. Now let's flip on back to our story with Mephibosheth and David.

Mephibosheth knows his family's history with King David. He also knows that David may see him as a threat. As the grandson of King Saul, he could argue for his right to be king. Is David looking to eliminate this threat? In the culture of that time, it was normal for a king to kill the whole family of a rival king, so you can imagine Mephibosheth's confusion at David's response.

Mephibosheth says, "Who am I that you pay attention to a stray dog like me?"

David calls King Saul's servant, Ziba, over and says, "Everything that belonged to Saul and his family, I've handed over to your master's grandson. You and your sons and your servants will work his land and bring in the produce for your master's grandson. Mephibosheth himself, your master's grandson, from now on will take all his meals at my table."

THE STORY WITHIN THE STORY

Mephibosheth's life had been a hard one. He fell as a child, causing him to be lame in both feet. His father died. His grandfather, King Saul, was disgraced and God replaced him with David. He lived in an obscure, forgotten place. We might say he was down and out; he was disgraced. And he'd been in hiding since he was five years old. Might King David find him any day now and put him in prison or, worse, take his life?

Would his life ever find meaning?

Imagine how Mephibosheth feels when the king summons him to appear in his palace. He knows that David and his grandfather, Saul, had a history that was anything but good. He has heard the stories of how Saul tried to kill David. So Mephibosheth is hiding out in Lo Debar, the wilderness, because he fears for his life. And in that fateful moment when he receives the news that King David wants to see him, he can only believe that his past has caught up with him.

How different the story turns out!

Instead of judgment or destruction, King David offers Mephibosheth a place at his table. Mephibosheth receives fellowship, food, and relationship from the king every day. Then David makes things even better. He restores Mephibosheth's property and even orders his land to be farmed and the income given to him.

After I read this story and considered its message, it

struck me. Mephibosheth's story is the same story the Bible tells—the story of the God King who seeks out the hopeless, those who are far away, and even his enemies and invites them into relationship with him at a personal cost to himself.

I really enjoy slowing down my reading of the Bible to gather all that's going on; Mephibosheth's story is an example of why.

THE BIG STORY

When you and I read these stories, it's good to remember to read them with the grand narrative of the Bible in view. This grand narrative is called a metanarrative. That's simply the overarching story told by the entirety of the Bible. Imagine the Bible as one long episodic story on television. Each week, you can tune in to watch the show. Each episode usually stands on its own. But each episode also contributes to the big story that's being told over the span of the whole season. You and I can't wait to watch the season finale, because we finally get some closure on the whole big story, or the metanarrative.

When I found Mephibosheth in my reading, I started asking questions.

Who was this lame man popping into the story?

Why was he important to the storyteller?

What does he add to the story of David's reign as king?

When I dug into these questions, I discovered that Mephibosheth not only contributed to the story of David by being a character who was connected to the previous king but also contributed to the metanarrative of the Bible and gave a very personal touch to the story of the creator God pursuing his creation and taking them into his presence.

Without knowing the larger story of the Bible, I easily could have overlooked Mephibosheth's story or considered it insignificant. But because I had a broader view of the Bible, I could see how Mephibosheth's story fit right in with the Bible's larger story.

The Bible's big picture includes the story of the God of creation ruling his realm, defending it against an archenemy bent on the destruction of mankind, and conquering evil by making a sacrifice that is the costliest the kingdom will ever know.

If all the stories are connected, and if knowing the big picture of the Bible helps us understand the individual stories of the Bible, then we should start our tour of the biblical story with an understanding of that big picture, and the best place to start is "In the beginning . . ."

THREE

IN THE BEGINNING

The story of the Bible begins with an incredible scene in which the whole world comes into existence through the words of God. The very first words of the Bible are, "In the beginning . . ." It almost sounds like, "Once upon a time . . ." or that song from *The Sound of Music* that begins, "Let's start at the very beginning, a very good place to start." And that's where the Bible's story starts, at the beginning—of everything. The dramatic opening line sets the stage. What happens next?

"In the beginning God created the heavens and the earth" (Gen. 1:1).

Let your mind run free for a moment. Remember, we

want to start from scratch. Don't get hung up on things you've heard people say about Genesis or about God. Let's just take the story at face value and try to enjoy it, like we would any good book or film.

This opening line works like a preface. It paints the scene for us. It gives us context for what is going on. We have this character, God. He has superpowers, as we would expect. The first superpower we see is his ability to create out of nothing. He creates this lump of clay called earth. This lump of clay is "formless and empty" (v. 2) and is covered in water and darkness. Talk about your dramatic and foreboding scenes. Can you picture it?

The mass of this earth is completely still, void of any tree or animal or mountain or river or sky or clouds or continents or people. It's empty. And not only is it empty, but you couldn't be on this planet if you wanted to. It's uninhabitable. Nothing on it could sustain life. And then God does something unexpected. He speaks to the blank canvas.

He's not your typical artist. He's not using oil or acrylic paints. He's not using textiles or watercolors. In fact, he's not using any kind of medium. He's using his voice.

Picture this. The earth and the heavens are there, but they are still very dark. There is just this kind of void. There's the earth and the heavens, but think of it. No stars. No sun. No moon. Nothing on the earth. The earth is still covered with darkness and water.

This God character is there, existing, hovering over this dark void. And then he speaks.

"God said, 'Let there be light,' and there was light. God saw that the light was good, and he separated the light from the darkness. God called the light 'day,' and the darkness he called 'night.' And there was evening, and there was morning—the first day" (vv. 3–5).

In these first verses of the Bible, we're ushered into a story in which a being called God creates with nothing but his words.

And not only does he create the heavens and the earth; he continues creating things. After the first day, he gets busy creating the sky. The Bible says that he separated the waters, creating a vault between them, which is another way to say he created the atmosphere, separating it from the water that was covering the earth.

On the third day, he really gets going. He speaks and the waters that were covering the whole earth gather in one place. He speaks again and the land appears. Oh, now he has his own kind of canvas, but one that he's spoken into existence. And what does he do? He speaks again and creates vegetation, seed-bearing plants and trees on the land. He wipes his hands together and says, "Nice. I think this will do." Well, he doesn't really say that. But he does call his work "good," or beautiful.

It's still kind of dark on day four, so he fixes that problem. He speaks: "Let there be lights in the vault of the sky to separate the day from the night, and let them serve as signs to mark sacred times, and days and years" (v. 14). God makes two great lights—one to govern the night, and the other to govern the day. Those would be the moon and the sun. Almost as an afterthought, the Bible adds, "He also made the stars" (v. 16).

On day five, God focuses on creating birds that will fly above the earth, as well as on filling the seas with living creatures. He makes all kinds of creatures to fill the great waters. And when he is done, again, he looks at all he has created in the air and in the seas, and he calls it beautiful.

The next day, he focuses on the land, creating livestock, creatures that walk the ground, and wild animals.

Then, on that same day, he makes mankind. God makes human beings in his own likeness, to rule over the creatures in the seas, the birds in the air, and the animals that walk on the land. He makes them male and female, and he tells them to multiply so they may fill the earth. He gives the man and woman the seed-bearing plants and trees as food.

Finally, when God has finished all this creating, he steps back, and he sees everything that he has done, and he says, "It is all very good."

Before we go on, for us to understand the story of the Bible, we need to remember the emphasis the story makes on this point. There are seven times in the first chapter of the Bible when it says what God created was "good," and the last time, it says God looked at all he made, and it was "very good." Because of what is about to happen, it is important to remember how the story started.

That's the first chapter of the book of Genesis, the first book in the Bible. Quite the beginning.

A RELATIONSHIP BETWEEN GOD AND MAN

In the second chapter of the Bible, the story gives more detail about the crowning achievement of God's creation. The Bible says God formed man out of the dust of the ground. And when he'd formed him, he breathed his own breath into his nostrils.

We were told in the first chapter that God said, "Let us make mankind in our image, in our likeness" (Gen. 1:26). In the creation story, only mankind—Adam and Eve— was created in God's image, and it was only with mankind that God "breathed into his nostrils the breath of life" (Gen. 2:7). This is what makes mankind unique in all of God's creation in the Bible's story. It was at that point that man became a living being.

First God made Adam. But then God looked at the man and said, "You know, it's not good for him to be alone. I'll make a suitable helper for him."

So God, who had created the birds and wild animals, brought them before the man to see what he would name them. And the man looked at each creature and named it.

And that's what they were called from then on. But after he finished naming the animals, no suitable helper was found for the man. This next part is pretty dreamy.

God caused Adam to fall asleep. And while he was asleep, God removed one of his ribs and formed a new creature.

Woman.

When Adam woke and saw the woman, he did the same thing he had done when he saw all the animals and birds parade before him. He named her. But this was very different. This time, he recognized this special gift, this partner given to him by God, and he named her, but not in the way you might think. In the Bible text, he says,

> "This is now bone of my bones
> and flesh of my flesh;
> she shall be called 'woman,'
> for she was taken out of man."
>
> —GENESIS 2:23

The story says that God placed them in a large garden in the east, in a place called Eden. God made beautiful plants and trees grow in the garden. The trees and shrubs were beautiful to look at and great for eating. In the middle of the garden, God created the tree of life and the tree of the knowledge of good and evil.

Adam and Eve didn't just spend their time wandering

around the garden gawking at all the beautiful scenery. God gave them a purpose. He wanted them to work the garden and keep watch over it. Mankind was meant to preserve the beauty of all God created. But Adam and Eve's main purpose was to be in the presence of God and to enjoy him.

They were intended to be with God and to follow the guidelines he set up for them in the garden. God gave them full rein over every living thing and told them they could eat from every tree and shrub in the garden. They just had to steer clear of one tree in Eden: the tree of the knowledge of good and evil. This one tree gave Adam and Eve a choice. They had the choice to obey or disobey. This was another thing that was unique to mankind. Only man, of all creation, was given this instruction; human beings alone were given moral choice.

"If you eat from it," God said, "you will die."

"Got it. All this I can eat. Stay away from that tree over there. Right."

But what did Adam and Eve think after God told them about the ramifications of eating from the tree? Did it surprise them? Frighten them? Did it ignite curiosity?

So there they were, Adam and Eve. The apex of God's creation. It was just God, Adam, and Eve, with all the animals. It reminds me of a Hallmark movie. Now, together, the man and woman lived in the garden. They served God there, and they enjoyed the great satisfaction of living in community with the Creator himself.

THE MESS OF SEPARATION FROM GOD

Here's where things fall apart. We're introduced to a fourth character in the story—the antagonist.

The serpent.

He approaches Eve and questions God's rules by asking Eve why she can't eat from the tree of the knowledge of good and evil.

"If we eat from that tree, we will die," Eve replies.

"What?" says the serpent. "No, you won't. God's just afraid that you will become like him—you'll know good from evil."

Eve looks at the fruit once again. It looks delightful, desirable. Besides, who wouldn't want to gain that kind of knowledge? The lure of wisdom is itself a strong and pleasing desire.

The next thing you know, Eve chooses to believe the serpent and eats the fruit. And then she shares it with her husband, Adam.

But what about God's rule, his warning to them?

What now?

This simple scene in which the serpent presents Eve with an alternative to God's command and encourages her to disobey God sets up the Bible story, an incredible narrative that unfolds throughout the rest of the book. Adam and Eve disobey God instead of believing him. They ignore God's words to them—words he meant for their protection, for he did not want them to die as a result of their disobedience.

God comes looking for Adam and Eve in the cool of one evening. He calls out to Adam. The two humans hear God coming through the wind, and they cover themselves with fig leaves and hide from the sight of God. It is a new response to God's presence. Never before have they felt compelled to cover their nakedness. Never before have they felt shame.

"Adam, where are you?" God asks.

Finally, Adam answers him. "We hid behind these trees because we were naked and afraid."

"Who told you that you were naked? Have you eaten from the tree that I told you not to eat from?"

Is God really wondering as to the whereabouts of Adam and Eve? Or is he sending them a signal: they're lost?

"The woman who you put with me here in the garden, she gave me some fruit from it, so I ate it."

"What is this you have done?" God asks Eve.

"The serpent deceived me, and I ate."

Then God turns his attention to the serpent.

It sets into motion the great epic rescue of God's creation by God himself. The story begins with delight but then ruin follows, like a scene out of a Shakespeare play. It sets the reader on a journey of discovery.

The journey is an odyssey in which God continues to deal with man. It's not always a pretty picture, and sometimes it's amazing. In the story of the Bible, God creates Adam and Eve so that they can be together, like a family. But when Adam and Eve choose their desires over God's, things change. The relationship is severed. As a result, God casts them out of the garden.

As for the serpent, he is cursed above all animals and livestock. He will crawl on his belly all his life, and he will contend with the offspring of the woman.

As for the woman, she will suffer greatly through childbearing. And there will be tension between her and her husband.

As for the man, he will find toil in his work; by the sweat of his brow he will get his food. God curses the ground because of Adam's disobedience. And when the man dies, he will return to the ground from which he was formed. So death becomes part of the Bible's story.

Because of their actions, Adam and Eve will live in a world estranged from God. And that's what the world becomes after they disobey: a world cursed by sin.

What will God do to get them back? What will need to happen in order for him to restore what has been lost?

After God expels Adam and Eve, he kills a couple of animals and makes clothes for them and sends them on their way. It's a sad moment for God. It wasn't his plan to send them away.

THE FALL

Many versions of the Bible, in the subheading of this chapter, refer to this garden scene as the fall.

After this first act of disobedience, we begin finding the word sin used more and more in the Bible story.

Before, when Adam and Eve lived happily in the garden and enjoyed the presence of God, they felt no guilt, no shame. There was no sin. There was true rest, pure delight. Only God. Remember, it was "very good." But then something else entered the picture: sin.

What is this word sin and how is it used in the Bible?

From the story, we see that sin is an act of disobedience that brings judgment. That's a very basic definition. And a great start. But as we will see as we get farther into the story, sin brings all kinds of havoc.

In the Bible's story, the penalty for sin is death. This is a recurring theme in the Bible, and we see sin's negative impact throughout the rest of the story. In the New Testament book of Romans, the writer, Paul, reiterates the consequence of sin by saying that the penalty for sin is death.

So how are people supposed to live?

The Bible says a person who has sinned is a guilty person, so that person needs to pay a penalty for their sin. We don't want to get ahead of ourselves, so for now, let's set this discussion of sin off to the side and continue with the story. We'll come back to it.

SPIRALING OUT OF CONTROL

After Adam and Eve leave the garden, Eve becomes pregnant and has her first son, Cain. Then Eve gives birth to Abel, her second son. Abel grows up to be a shepherd, and

Cain grows up to be a farmer. When it is time to bring their offerings from their work to God, Abel's sacrifice finds favor in God's sight, but Cain's does not.

Cain is upset. He worked hard and offered what he had, but it was not found favorable to God. God comes to Cain and asks him, "Why are you so upset, Cain? Why so angry? If you do what is right, you know that you will be accepted, right? But"—God warns him—"if you do not do what is right, sin is crouching at your door; it wants to have you, but you must control it." And just like that, we're talking about sin again. It never stays out of the discussion very long.

Later on, Cain invites his brother for a walk out in the fields. They don't talk very much, because once they reach the fields, Cain attacks Abel and kills him. It's the first murder in the Bible.

God comes looking for Cain, just like he came looking for Adam and Eve.

"Where is your brother, Abel?"

"I don't know. Am I my brother's keeper?" Cain shoots back at God.

Have you ever heard someone say that line, "Am I my brother's keeper?"

It is a common phrase, like so many others that come from the Bible.

"What have you done?" exclaims God. "Listen! Your brother's blood cries out to me from the ground" (Gen. 4:10–11).

Cain sinned. He didn't heed God's warning that sin was waiting for him. In his anger, he chose his desire to harm Abel because of his jealousy and killed his own brother—an act that exposes his heart and brings on guilt that needs to be punished. So God punishes him.

Then, for a while, things in this newly created world seem to settle down, and as Adam and Eve continue to have children and populate the earth, "people [begin] to call on the name of the LORD" (v. 26).

But things don't stay like that for long. Soon sin and violence begin to take over, so much so that the Bible says that every thought of mankind was evil and the earth was filled with violence. God thinks that he should destroy the earth. But before he does, he finds one good person. His name is Noah, and because of the wickedness of man, God tells Noah that he is going to destroy the earth with water and instructs Noah to build a boat.

"A boat?" says Noah.

"Yes," replies God.

Then God tells him exactly how to build it. God also wants to save the animals. So he causes the animals to gather to Noah before the floods come—a pair of every creature and seven pairs of what the Bible calls "clean" animals, like cows, deer, goats, and sheep (see Leviticus 11).

This is a well-known story from the Bible that is told in children's books and Hollywood movies. There are even recreations of the ark, using the dimensions given in the Bible. One is in Kentucky.

As the story of Noah goes, "the springs of the great deep burst forth, and the floodgates of the heavens were opened" (Gen. 7:11). Rain continues for forty days and forty nights, till all the earth is covered in water. As a result of the flood, all of mankind and all the land animals and birds of the air die.

After forty days and forty nights, God sends a wind to dry up the waters so that the ark rests on dry ground. Then God tells Noah to come out of the ark. Noah and his family, and all of the paired animals, embark on a journey into the new world—well, new world post-flood. The first thing Noah does? He builds an altar and sacrifices burnt offerings to God. God is pleased with the offering and reflects on the circumstance "in his heart" (Gen. 8:21).

"Never again," God says to himself, "will I curse the ground because of humans, even though every inclination of the human heart is evil from childhood. And never again will I destroy all living creatures, as I have done.

> "As long as the earth endures,
> seedtime and harvest,
> cold and heat,
> summer and winter,
> day and night
> will never cease."
>
> —GENESIS 8:21–22

After his moment of reflection, God sets a rainbow in the sky as a promise to Noah and his descendants. Never again will God destroy the earth by a flood. God's promise to Noah is referred to in the Bible as a covenant. We will see more of God's covenants with human beings throughout the biblical story. God tells Noah, "I have set my rainbow in the clouds, and it will be the sign of the covenant between me and the earth. Whenever I bring clouds over the earth and the rainbow appears in the clouds, I will remember my covenant between me and you and all living creatures of every kind. Never again will the waters become a flood to destroy all life. Whenever the rainbow appears in the clouds, I will see it and remember the everlasting covenant between God and all living creatures of every kind on the earth" (Gen. 9:13–16).

God also says something familiar. He tells Noah and his family to "be fruitful and increase in number; multiply on the earth and increase upon it" (v. 7). Remember when he told Adam and Eve the same thing? And so the world starts over.

So then what happens?

Do Noah and his family live happily ever after?

Unfortunately, they do not.

Man continues to have a sin problem.

As good as Noah is, sin shows up in him and his family. Not through a clever serpent. This time, the humans don't need coaxing.

The genealogy portions of the Bible are considered some of the most boring parts. *The Prayer of Jabez*, written by Bruce Wilkinson in 2000, was a bestseller, and it came from the genealogy in the Old Testament book of 1 Chronicles. In the midst of the genealogy, the writer includes a prayer by one of the descendants, Jabez: "Jabez cried out to the God of Israel, 'Oh, that you would bless me and enlarge my territory! Let your hand be with me, and keep me from harm so that I will be free from pain.' And God granted his request" (1 Chron. 4:10).

Wilkinson made this genealogy famous. But genealogies serve a bigger purpose in the biblical narrative. The Bible is connected throughout by genealogies. In Genesis, we discover two of several genealogies in the Bible. Here I've broken down the ages of characters mentioned in chapters 5 and 11 of Genesis. The first thing you will notice is the age of the men listed. It shows they regularly lived more than 900 years. Here's how Genesis 5:3–5 puts it: "When Adam had lived 130 years, he had a son in his own likeness, in his own image; and he named him Seth. After Seth was born, Adam lived 800 years and had other sons and daughters. Altogether, Adam lived a total of 930 years, and then he died."

The Bible proceeds to give similar information on a line of descendants from Adam. Here is a summary of the verses from Genesis 5:3–32.

Adam	130	Seth	+ 800 = 930
Seth	105	Enosh	+ 807 = 912

Enosh	90	Kenan	+ 815 = 905
Kenan	70	Mahalalel	+ 840 = 910
Mahalalel	65	Jared	+ 830 = 895
Jared	162	Enoch	+ 800 = 962
Enoch	65	Methuselah	+ 300 = 365
Methuselah	187	Lamech	+ 782 = 969
Lamech	182	Noah	+ 595 = 777
Noah	500	Shem, Ham, Japheth	Noah lived 950 years (Gen. 9:29)

The genealogies continue in Genesis 11. We aren't told the age of Noah when Shem was born, but other dating seems to indicate that Noah was 502 at that time. With that estimate, we continue the chart.

Noah	502	Shem	+ 448 = 950
Shem	100	Arphaxad	+ 500 = 600
Arphaxad	35	Shelah	+ 403 = 438
Shelah	30	Eber	+ 403 = 433
Eber	34	Peleg	+ 430 = 464

Peleg	30	Reu	+ 209 = 239
Reu	32	Serug	+ 207 = 239
Serug	30	Nahor	+ 200 = 230
Nahor	29	Terah	+ 119 = 148
Terah	70	Abraham, Nahor, Haran	

Let's think through some of these numbers. To determine how old Adam was when Methuselah was born, add the numbers in the first column from Adam to Enoch. This would indicate that Adam was around 687 years old when Methuselah was born. Methuselah is the oldest person recorded in the Bible, living to the age of 969. Genesis says Adam lived to be 930 years old. Therefore Methuselah was around 243 years old when Adam died. Methuselah is shown to be 369 years old when Noah was born, and we're told he lived 600 years after Noah was born. Methuselah is Noah's grandfather and lived 243 years while Adam was alive and 600 years after Noah was born. We are not told whether Methuselah knew either Adam or Noah, but he would have lived during both of their lifetimes. Now, that's some long living!

The same could be said of Noah's father, Lamech, who would have been 56 years old when Adam died.

The text does not reveal the age of Terah when Abraham was born, just that when he was 70, he had children, Abraham being one of those. Since Noah lived to be 950 years old, he must have died after Terah started to have children, so Noah would have been alive during Abraham's father's life. When you put all that together, it means Adam could have known Methuselah, who could have known Noah, who could have known Terah, Abraham's father. There are only four layers of separation between Adam and Abraham, the father of the Jewish nation. To Abraham, the flood and creation accounts would not have been folklore or legends passed down over twenty generations. They could be first- and second-hand accounts passed from Methuselah and Noah to his father, Terah. Okay, so maybe that is not what you were wondering when you picked up this book, but I find it interesting.

The downward spiral of separation from God continued with the introduction of the city called Babel. At this time, the Bible says, all the people on earth spoke in one common language. And many of them settled in a place called the plain of Shinar. There they developed ways to make structures, not with stones but with bricks made out of mud and dried in the sun. As the city developed, the people wanted to make a name for themselves, and they began to build a tower to the heavens.

Remember how God walked with Adam and Eve in

the garden? Well, God visited Babel. "The LORD came down to see the city and the tower the people were building" (Gen. 11:5). Again God reflected on the situation: "If all the people continue to share a language, then this will be only the beginning." God confused their language so that they could not understand each other. This state of confusion is where the city gets its name.

The story of Babel ends the foundation of the Bible. After this story, the narrative shifts its focus onto a person and his descendants, a person on whom the rest of the biblical story is built. That person is a man called Abram, whose name God eventually changes to Abraham. If you recall, this is the first person in the timeline laid out in the introduction. He enters the Bible story around 2000 BC.

A BRIEF REVIEW

Before we go on, let's review the story up to this point.

The opening character of the Bible's story, God, creates all things and calls his creation very good. Adam and Eve are unique in all of God's creation. We are told that man and woman are created in the image of God and that they are given the choice to obey, are given work to do, and are given dominion over the rest of creation. As a result of the disobedience of humans, sin enters the story, and we see the consequences that follow. Sin breaks the relationship man had with God, death becomes a reality, and evil becomes a part of all mankind.

There is a series of questions God has begun to answer, which are part of the story.

What is man going to do now that he has been
   thrown out of the garden?
Will his relationship with God ever be restored?
Can mankind fix the problem?
What will God do?
Does he give up on mankind?
Does he fix the problem?

As with any good story, these questions keep us turning the pages.

DIGGING INTO THE CHARACTERS

When I read a story, I love to discover more about the main characters. The more we know the characters, the better we understand their motivation for their actions. And the more we know about them, the closer we get to them. We either root for them or love to hate them.

Who are these characters of ours? We've already met some of them.

There's this God figure, then Adam and Eve, and then there's the crafty serpent.

When I read the beginning of Genesis, I get enthralled with the character of God. Who is he, really? And why does he like humans so much? And what's his relationship with the serpent?

I've found that the more I dig around regarding this God figure, the clearer the story of the Bible becomes.

FOUR

LETTING GOD
BE GOD

In the musical *Les Misérables*, I had a hard time keeping the characters straight. It was hard for me to tell who was the good guy and who was the bad guy. But once I got to know the main characters, everything else began to follow.

The more we know the characters, the better we understand the motivation for their actions. And the more we know about them, the better connected we feel to them.

Let's take a brief look at two of the easiest characters first: Adam and Eve.

What do we know about them so far? Well, they are human. They have a command from God, and they disobey that command. God expels them from the garden. We understand Adam and Eve. We all know what it is like to disobey.

The Bible goes on to explain that now all of Adam and Eve's descendants will struggle with the same "sin and disobedience" problem. Now Adam and Eve and their descendants will struggle, and all of mankind will live separated from God. The intended relationship with God is lost—for the moment.

This lost relationship becomes the key problem addressed in the rest of the Bible. How will man's relationship with God get restored? Or perhaps stated more colorfully, how does man get back to Eden?

Both the Old and the New Testaments mention the problem of being separated from God. The Old Testament book of Psalms says,

> God looks down from heaven
>   on all mankind
> to see if there are any who understand,
>   any who seek God.
> Everyone has turned away, all have become
>   corrupt;

there is no one who does good,

not even one.

—PSALM 53:2–3

Then, in the New Testament book of Romans, the writer quotes this very psalm:

As it is written:

"None is righteous, no, not one;
no one understands;
no one seeks for God.
All have turned aside; together they have become
worthless;
no one does good,
not even one."

—ROMANS 3:10–12 ESV

The passage states that no one possesses the ability to be righteous, and "no one seeks for God" (v. 11 ESV). That's how the Bible describes mankind—lost, faraway, with shame. Just like Mephibosheth.

Undergirding the story of this beautiful book is that question: how can the relationship man had with his Creator be restored? To answer that question, the story of the Bible turns to *the* main character: God.

How do you understand the God of the Bible? Many

have imposed their understanding of who God is, but let's pause for a moment and ask, what does the Bible say about this main character?

GOD IS A CREATOR

Remember that first line to the whole story? "In the beginning God created the heavens and the earth" (Gen. 1:1). This first line introduces us to God.

But who *is* he?

Where did he come from?

What kinds of powers does he have?

How does he relate to his creation?

For our little journey through the Bible's story, we simply want to look at what the Bible says about God.

This first line describes God as a creator. Throughout the Bible, this aspect of God surfaces. The book of Psalms says, "May you be blessed by the LORD, the Maker of heaven and earth" (Ps. 115:15).

The Old Testament book of Isaiah says, "LORD Almighty, the God of Israel, enthroned between the cherubim, you alone are God over all the kingdoms of the earth. You have made heaven and earth" (Isa. 37:16).

Returning to the New Testament, in the book of Acts we find a prayer to God that begins with, "When they heard this, they raised their voices together in prayer to God. 'Sovereign Lord,' they said, 'you made the heavens and the earth and the sea, and everything in them'" (Acts 4:24).

In the last book of the Bible, Revelation, a verse refers to God as creator when it says, "[An angel] said in a loud voice, 'Fear God and give him glory, because the hour of his judgment has come. Worship him who made the heavens, the earth, the sea and the springs of water'" (Rev. 14:7).

In the Bible, we read verses like the one from the Old Testament prophet Jeremiah, who says of God, "Ah, Sovereign LORD, you have made the heavens and the earth by your great power and outstretched arm. Nothing is too hard for you" (Jer. 32:17). In essence, the Bible here describes God as all-powerful.

The Bible also describes God as being everywhere, by using the word spirit. In the Psalms, God is asked a rhetorical question: "Where can I go from your Spirit? Where can I flee from your presence?" (Ps. 139:7). This indicates that God's Spirit is everywhere.

Jeremiah records God as saying, "Do not I fill heaven and earth?" (Jer. 23:24).

So God is all-powerful, and he is a spirit who is everywhere. But that's not all. The Bible also says that God possesses all knowledge. In the Psalms, we find this statement.

> You have searched me, LORD,
>   and you know me.
> You know when I sit and when I rise;
>   you perceive my thoughts from afar.
> You discern my going out and my lying down;
>   you are familiar with all my ways.

> Before a word is on my tongue
>> you, LORD, know it completely.
> You hem me in behind and before,
>> and you lay your hand upon me.
> Such knowledge is too wonderful for me,
>> too lofty for me to attain.
>
> —PSALM 139:1–6

The New Testament book of Romans says, "Oh, the depth of the riches and wisdom and knowledge of God! How unsearchable are his judgments and how inscrutable his ways!" (Rom. 11:33 ESV).

Okay, quick recap. Thematically and throughout, the Bible describes God as being everywhere, all-powerful, and all-knowing. It says God is bigger and better than anything else—as in Isaiah, in which we find God describing himself like this: "As the heavens are higher than the earth, so are my ways higher than your ways and my thoughts than your thoughts" (Isa. 55:9).

The God of the Bible exists on a different plane than does his creation. He can't be figured out; he's sort of a mystery that can't be fully understood.

GOD IS LOVE

While the God of the Bible is described as a true God, there is another prominent aspect of him found throughout the biblical narrative. Sometimes this aspect is stated boldly and plainly. Sometimes it is whispered. In the New Testament book of 1 John, the author puts it bluntly: "God is love" (1 John 4:16).

He is love. He's not mad or vengeful. This may not be the most common characteristic of *a* god or gods portrayed on television or in the movies, but it is how the God of the Bible is described.

One of the most well-known verses of the Bible makes that point. John 3:16 says, "God so *loved* the world that he gave his one and only Son, that whoever believes in him shall not perish but have eternal life" (emphasis added). Not only is God love, but he loves his creation.

Perhaps you recognize this verse. It's popular in our culture, as it's been plastered on bumper stickers, billboards, and signs at sporting events. People sometimes wear it as jewelry and tattoo it on their skin. They also embroider it on hats and shirts and put it just about anyplace you can think of. This is, for many children who attend church, among the first verses they are encouraged to memorize.

The writer of Psalm 136 also says God is good and that his love lasts forever. Twenty-six times, the poet says, "His love endures forever." Why? Because he *is* love.

This aspect of the God of the Bible adds to the story of the Bible. Remember the falling out between God and his creation, Adam and Eve? Their relationship was broken. Isn't it intriguing to wonder how a loving God will respond to his wayward creation? If he is a God of love, does he give up on his creation, or is there a way to restore the relationship?

This brings us to another aspect of this character, God: he is said to be a God of mercy.

A GOD OF MERCY

Creative.

Omnipresent.

All-powerful.

All-knowing.

Loving.

Those are powerful traits, and yet there is still more. The Bible also refers to God as merciful—a God ready to forgive and full of compassion.

In the book of Nehemiah, the writer remembers a time when God's people were acting stubbornly. Nehemiah says, "In your great mercy you did not put an end to them or abandon them, for you are a gracious and merciful God" (Neh. 9:31). In describing God's mercy, the Bible says God is "gracious and compassionate, slow to anger and rich in love" (Ps. 145:8).

On Mount Sinai, God describes himself to Moses, one of our key characters, as merciful. On several occasions in the book of Psalms, a form of the word merciful is used to describe God. The book of Joel says, "Return to the LORD your God, for he is gracious and compassionate, slow to anger and abounding in love, and he relents from sending calamity" (Joel 2:13).

Then, in the New Testament books of James, Ephesians, and 1 Peter, the writers describe God as "full of mercy" (James 3:17), "rich in mercy" (Eph. 2:4), and having "great mercy" (1 Peter 1:3).

These aspects of love and mercy share a common bond because it's hard to distinguish one from the other. Part of being a loving person is being merciful—able and willing to show compassion and forgive. They go hand in hand, and the Bible ascribes both characteristics to God.

GOD IS HOLY

The Bible describes God as holy. That means God is unlike his creation. His creation is now mired in sin that separates them from their creator God.

The word holy means that God is morally perfect, totally pure; there is no imperfection in him at all. God even instructs his creation to be holy.

God says this in the Old Testament book of Leviticus: "I am the LORD your God; consecrate yourselves and be holy, because I am holy" (Lev. 11:44).

But how could his creation be holy like God? After all, mankind disobeyed God and decided to follow their own path, as we discovered earlier. How was this fallen man supposed to understand this word holiness?

There's a story in the book of Isaiah, chapter 6, that describes the power of God's holiness. I think this story will help flesh out the characteristic of holiness. Remember, Isaiah is one of the main characters in our timeline.

Isaiah, who was a prophet from Israel (we'll discuss prophets a bit farther into our journey), writes about a vision of God he experienced. In the vision, Isaiah finds himself in the presence of God, who is sitting in heaven on a throne. God wears an enormous robe that fills the temple. Above God stand the seraphim. Not a seraphim or a few seraphim but *the* seraphim. They're described by Isaiah as six-winged angels; one set of wings covers their faces, another set covers their feet, while the final set is used for flying. Talk about a crazy dream.

Picture a crowd of these multiwinged angels called seraphim—because we're not told exactly how many—hovering above God as he's seated on a throne in the temple of heaven, his robe billowing all around, filling the temple. The seraphim call out to one another, saying, "Holy, holy, holy is the LORD Almighty; the whole earth is full of his glory" (Isa. 6:3).

The voices of the seraphim shake the doorposts of the temple, and smoke fills the room. Isaiah realizes he's in the presence of the creator God and knows he's in trouble and calls out, "Woe to me! . . . I am ruined! For I am a man of unclean lips, and I live among a people of unclean lips, and my eyes have seen the King, the LORD Almighty" (v. 5).

In this scene, the writer shows us a picture of the

contrast between God and man. Isaiah feels immense concern as he comes before the holy God. Why? Because of his "unclean lips," which is another way to describe his own sin, or his uncleanness. When he finds himself in the presence of the holy God, he feels as though his sin is exposed for what it is.

The story continues.

One of the seraphim takes a set of tongs and picks up one of the coals from the fire and flies to Isaiah and touches his lips with the burning coal. The seraphim says, "See, this has touched your lips; your guilt is taken away and your sin atoned for" (v. 7).

In this vision, the problem of Isaiah's self-described sin is removed by the mere touching of his lips with the glowing coal, and his guilt is "atoned for," as the writer says. While this was just a vision, the question remains: is there a way for the sin of mankind to be taken away? It's a mind-bending scene, filled with mystery and fantastic images. And in the story, it provides the reader with a glimpse of hope.

Elsewhere in the Bible, we find a structure called the tabernacle. As the Bible describes the tabernacle, another example of God's holiness is apparent. The tabernacle represents God's dwelling place.

One of our main characters, Moses, is taking the Israelites from Egypt to Canaan. We will look closer at that story later. The journey takes forty years, and during the journey they are instructed by God to build a mobile tabernacle, or tent, as a place for God to dwell. There are specific instructions on how the tent is to be built.

Later in the nation of Israel's history, a permanent form of the tabernacle, called the temple, is built by King Solomon, the son of King David, another of our main characters. That temple is referred to as Solomon's Temple, or the First Temple. The Bible records its destruction by Nebuchadnezzar, the king of Babylon, and its reconstruction through the direction of Cyrus, the king of Persia. The rebuilt temple is referred to as the Second Temple. This temple was destroyed by the Romans in AD 70. Today if you visit Jerusalem, you can visit the Wailing Wall, which is the remains of this Second Temple.

Picture this in your mind: Inside the tabernacle, as you entered, there was an outer area, followed by two inner areas—the Holy Place, and then the innermost area, which was called the Holy of Holies. The Holy of Holies was a place for God to dwell.

Only a priest was allowed to enter the Holy of Holies, because of mankind's sin. And he had to offer a sacrifice to atone for that sin problem. He did this by offering an animal. Remember how awestruck and even frightened Isaiah was when he found himself in the presence of God? Well, the priests also understood that being in the presence of God was an intense and potentially dangerous ordeal.

If the priest had not properly cleansed himself, which represented atoning for his sins, then his uncleanness would cause him to die in the presence of God—because, remember, God is holy. In the New Testament, John says, "God is light; in him there is no darkness" (1 John 1:5). Think about it like this: the priest's sin was darkness, and because God's holiness is pure light, it cannot tolerate darkness of any kind.

A GOD OF JUSTICE

Love.

Mercy.

Holiness.

And now justice.

In the Old Testament book of Deuteronomy, Moses, just before his death, writes what the Bible refers to as a song.

In the song, he describes God as the Rock. The song reads, "His works are perfect, and all his ways are just. A faithful God who does no wrong, upright and just is he" (Deut. 32:4).

In the last book of the Bible, Revelation, we find another writer recounting a vision of God. The vision includes a group of people in heaven singing the song of Moses. Here is what it says.

> "Great and marvelous are your deeds,
>> Lord God Almighty.
> Just and true are your ways,
>> King of the nations.

Who will not fear you, Lord,
    and bring glory to your name?
For you alone are holy.
All nations will come
    and worship before you,
for your righteous acts have been revealed."

                       —REVELATION 15:3–4

Here the Bible describes God's ways as just *and* holy. This presents an interesting contrast of God's character. On one hand, he is loving and merciful, but on the other hand, he is holy and just.

If you remember back to the story of Noah and the flood, we're told that because of the wickedness and violence of man, God was going to destroy everyone. Why in the world would God destroy human beings?

Time and time again in the Bible, we discover that God's holiness requires wickedness to be punished. And yet even though his holiness requires this, we also find that his love and mercy provide a way for his creation to start all over again—a new beginning. In the story of the flood, the ark was the way of escape for Noah and his family. God loved and showed mercy on his creation through the ark.

So this God is holy and just, which requires a penalty for the sin of mankind. I understood this concept as a son and understand it even better now as a father. When my children disobeyed when they were younger, they realized there was a consequence for their action. But they also rested in the knowledge that their father would forgive them and offer mercy when they recognized what they had done and were sorry for messing up.

God is also merciful and loving, which provides a way of escape for mankind. Let's look at how one writer illustrates a similar paradox in one of his characters.

THE NATURES OF LIONS AND GODS

You may be familiar with the book by the popular writer C. S. Lewis titled *The Lion, The Witch and the Wardrobe*. It was made into a movie in 2005. Lewis's now-famous character Aslan is a good example of this paradox, as Lewis portrays him as being dangerous but merciful.

When the Pevensie children find their way into Narnia through the wardrobe, they happen upon Mr. Beaver. Mr. Beaver takes the children to his humble home and tells them the story about the White Witch's curse on Narnia, which makes it always winter but never Christmas. But Mr. Beaver adds a dash of hope to the story when he tells the children that Aslan is on the move.

When the children hear the name Aslan, they each feel something very good and wonderful rise up inside them, just at the mention of his name. When Mr. Beaver says they must travel to see Aslan, the children are surprised to hear that Aslan is a lion. The oldest sister, Susan, asks if he is safe.

Mr. Beaver replies with the memorable line, "Safe? Who said anything about safe? 'Course he isn't safe. But he's good. He's the King, I tell you."

Aslan is a lion. So, naturally, he by his own lion nature would not be considered safe. But the caveat? He is good. There's a bit of unpredictability with this lion because, even though in the story he talks and is the true king of Narnia, there are no guarantees that he will even come close to meeting our expectations of him. Lions are dangerous and ferocious and greatly feared because of their nature. But the beauty of Aslan's character lies in his contrasting character: he's a *good* lion, but a lion nonetheless. Though he is good, one must never forget that he also possesses the power of a lion and the nature of a lion.

There's a scene in C. S. Lewis's *The Silver Chair*, book four in the Chronicles of Narnia, in which one of the characters, a little girl named Jill, desperately needs something to drink from the stream. But Aslan sits by the stream, and she doesn't know what to do with a massive lion sitting there.

She's afraid.

Jill asks Aslan if he could move on from the stream. Naturally, she's uncomfortable. But Aslan refuses. Then Jill asks if there's another stream to drink from, but Aslan assures her that this is the only stream. If she doesn't want to die of thirst, she will have to drink in the presence of the great lion. Then Jill asks if Aslan will promise not to eat her, but the lion laughs and does not promise. He's consumed many things in this world, including young girls, he reminds her. He's a lion; it's his nature to consume things. Aslan again reminds Jill, and us the readers, that he acts in a consistent way, according to his character. Jill drinks from the stream in the lion's presence and discovers him to be both terrifying and calming.

Lewis did a good job of showing how one character can possess two contrasting characteristics. This little snippet is an effort to help us envision the shape of this God character.

In such a short time, it's impossible to say all that could be said about God. He's a complex character, as we've seen just by surveying a few of his characteristics. He is described as being far beyond human comprehension, yet we are told he is both loving and holy at the same time.

The most important thing to keep in mind as we continue on with the story of the Bible is that the Bible calls the creator God good. Psalm 86:15 puts it this way: "You, Lord, are a compassionate and gracious God, slow to anger, abounding in love and faithfulness."

Now let's jump back into the story.

FIVE

GOD'S RESCUE PLAN: PART 1

The story picks back up in Genesis chapter 12 with Abram. Abram enters the biblical narrative during a rough time in the world. To understand Abram's role, let's give a quick recap of the events preceding his life. Remember, after God created the world, this thing called sin entered the world because that sly serpent convinced Adam and Eve that they would not die when they ate the forbidden fruit. Giving in to their desire to be like God led to their disobedience. This started a chain of events, the first being their ejection from the garden of Eden. They then lived separated from God.

The consequences of Adam and Eve's disobedience carries over to all mankind. Soon we witness the first murder in the story, with Cain killing his brother Abel out of jealousy. Later, Lamech, a son of Cain, murders a man and boasts about it. People become increasingly evil until, finally, God rethinks his decision to create the world and decides to send a flood to destroy it. But he finds one good man, Noah, and his family and instructs him to build an ark so that they can survive the cataclysmic flood, along with all the animals.

After forty days and forty nights of living through the floodwaters, Noah and his family help God reboot the world. But again man falls. In their pride, the people of Shinar build a great tower, wanting to make a name for themselves. God confuses their language so that they can no longer work together. That was the Tower of Babel story. Evil reigns in the hearts of the human race, and now confusion among the peoples of the world disperses them all over the land. Though the flood provided humanity with a fresh start, it didn't solve the heart problem. What will bring back the communion between God and man?

GOD MAKES A FRIEND

Now we meet Abram, our first main character in this part of the story.

Abram arrives on the scene, in chapter 12 of Genesis, when the world's been tossed into confusion; it's one big mess. The Bible narrative turns from a chronological focus to the focus on one man and his family. And that is Abram, descended from the family of Shem, one of Noah's three sons. But when Abram enters the narrative, the history of the world has come several generations from Shem—about four hundred years' worth, give or take (Gen. 11:10–32).

God comes to Abram, who has settled in Harran with his wife, Sarai, and tells him to leave his homeland and go "to the land I will show you" (Gen. 12:1). So Abram obeys God and leaves. He takes his wife and his nephew Lot and all of his possessions. It's here in the biblical story where we come across another covenant, or promise.

Remember, God's promise to Noah was never to flood the earth again, and he set a rainbow in the sky to seal the commitment.

God also makes a covenant with Abram. He promises Abram that his descendants will become a great nation and that the world will be blessed through them.

> "I will make you into a great nation,
>   and I will bless you;
> I will make your name great,
>   and you will be a blessing.
> I will bless those who bless you,
>   and whoever curses you I will curse;
> and all peoples on earth
>   will be blessed through you."
> —GENESIS 12:2–3

The whole promise sounds incredible. Through Abram's family, God will bless the entire world! Things are looking up for the human race. Maybe this sin problem can be fixed; who knows?

Books on the life and times of Abram could be written. There's so much to be told. But we don't have the space here to include all of his story. So to keep things moving, let's go to one of the most important episodes in Abram's life.

Abram gets old, and he and his wife, Sarai, still don't have a child to carry on their name. How will God's promise come true? Abram asks God this very question: "Sovereign LORD, what can you give me since I remain childless and the one who will inherit my estate is Eliezer of Damascus? . . . You have given me no children; so a servant in my household will be my heir" (Gen. 15:2–3).

God reiterates his promise to Abram and tells him his descendants will be as numerous as the stars. "This man will not be your heir, but a son who is your own flesh and blood will be your heir" (v. 4). He takes Abram outside and says, "Look up at the sky and count the stars—if indeed you can count them" (v. 5). Then God says to him, "So shall your offspring be" (v. 5).

God also tells Abram that he will give him a land: "I am the LORD, who brought you out of Ur of the Chaldeans to give you this land to take possession of it" (v. 7). Abram then falls into a deep sleep, and God speaks to him. I'm hesitant to share all that God tells Abram in the dream, because—I have to be honest—it contains a spoiler. But I'm going to go ahead and tell you this one thing God says to Abram.

> "Know for certain that for four hundred years your descendants will be strangers in a country not their own and that they will be enslaved and mistreated there. But I will punish the nation they serve as slaves, and afterward they will come out with great possessions. You, however, will go to your ancestors in peace and be buried at a good old age. In the fourth generation your descendants will come back here, for the sin of the Amorites has not yet reached its full measure."
>
> —GENESIS 15:13–16

What is this all about?

Well, this is God predicting the future for Abram. It's included in the story, and as we read it, we don't know exactly why God communicates this to Abram, but it's there, and we keep reading. Let's keep this foretelling of future events in our minds. We'll come to it again.

Finally, in their old age, Abram and his wife have a son, and they name him Isaac. It's an old-age miracle! Really old—Abram is one hundred and Sarai is eighty when Isaac is born. God has kept his promise, at least the first part of it, so far. Now the story of Abram really begins to unfold. God changes Abram's name to Abraham, and then we learn all about his son Isaac.

Isaac marries a woman named Rebecca, and they have twins—two boys. The oldest they name Esau, and the youngest they name Jacob. Jacob negotiates for his brother's birthright—in those days, the oldest sibling inherited a larger portion of the father's estate—and then steals his brother's blessing by deceiving their father. Esau is enraged with Jacob, but Jacob leaves town. In his travels, Jacob has a number of memorable experiences, including a crazy dream of a stairway to heaven, and then later on, after he establishes a family, he wrestles a man who is referred to as God.

Jacob and God wrestle throughout the night, but Jacob does not give up, even when the man asks him to. So the man touches him in the hip, which injures Jacob and causes him to limp. When the wrestling match ends at dawn, God renames Jacob. He names him Israel, which means "one who wrestles with God." Throughout the rest of the Bible, he is often still referred to as Jacob, while his children are referred to as the children of Israel and the nation is called Israel. This name change is also where the modern-day nation of Israel gets its name.

I told you Abraham's family stories were crazy.

Jacob has many sons. The story of how he has so many sons is an epic all on its own. And though I can't do it justice here, let me draw a little sketch of it.

Jacob falls in love with a beautiful woman named

Rachel—she is one of the few people in all of the Bible to be described as beautiful—and asks her father, Laban, for her hand in marriage. Laban agrees but requires seven years of work from Jacob in return.

Jacob agrees to work the seven years for Laban in exchange for Rachel's hand, because Jacob adores her. Rachel is his heart. And so time ticks away.

Seven years later, Jacob is finally united with the woman he loves. But on their wedding night, Laban tricks Jacob and sends his oldest daughter, Leah, into the tent instead of Rachel. It's dark in the tent, and Jacob doesn't know that it's Leah. When Jacob wakes the next morning, he is furious.

"Why did you do this?" he asks Laban.

"Because it's our custom to marry the oldest daughter before the youngest."

Jacob agrees to work for Laban another seven years for Rachel. Now he has two wives, to each of whom Laban has given a maidservant. Zilpah is the maidservant to Leah, and Bilhah is the maidservant to Rachel. Whew. Are you keeping up?

At first, Rachel can't have children; she's barren. But Leah can. We read about jealousy between the two sisters. It's a tense situation. This leads Rachel to give her maidservant, Bilhah, to Jacob to bear children for her, which in turn leads Leah to give Jacob her maidservant, Zilpah, to bear children for her. Rachel eventually has two boys of her own. All totaled, Leah produces seven children—six boys and a girl named Dinah. Bilhah, Zilpah, and Rachel each have two boys. To simplify things, here's a list of the sons of Jacob and their mothers, in birth order.

Sons of Leah: Reuben (the firstborn), Simeon, Levi, Judah
Sons of Rachel's servant Bilhah: Dan and Naphtali
Sons of Leah's servant Zilpah: Gad and Asher
Sons of Leah: Issachar and Zebulun
Sons of Rachel: Joseph and Benjamin (the youngest brother)

To say this is a dysfunctional household is an understatement. But so the story goes. This is the house of Israel, and the descendants of Abraham.

Before Jacob's family becomes a nation at the end of Genesis and the beginning of Exodus—the second book of the Bible—the family finds themselves in Egypt.

How did they get there?

We have to read the story of Joseph to learn about Egypt becoming home for Jacob's family.

Have you ever heard of the story of Joseph and his coat of many colors? Many years ago, there was a Broadway musical called *Joseph and the Amazing Technicolor Dreamcoat.* It's based on the biblical story of Joseph.

The Bible tells the story of how Joseph was a young dreamer and how his father, Jacob, favored him above his older brothers. The story takes up more than 30 percent of the book of Genesis. It's a pivotal story because it sets the stage for our next major character. So let's look at Joseph's story.

A DREAMER AND A BETRAYAL

Joseph was seventeen years old and Jacob's favorite son because he and his brother Benjamin were the two sons of the love of his life, Rachel. Plus Rachel had died giving birth to Benjamin, so there was an emotional tie to these two young boys. Joseph dreamed many dreams—strange dreams, like his father had. He told his father and his brothers about two of his dreams, in which he was set in charge of the whole family. "Listen to this dream I had," said Joseph. "We were binding sheaves of grain out in the field when suddenly my sheaf rose and stood upright, while your sheaves gathered around mine and bowed down to it" (Gen. 37:6–7).

The second dream was more of the same. "Listen," he said, "I had another dream, and this time the sun and moon and eleven stars were bowing down to me" (Gen. 37:9).

His brothers didn't like either dream. They hated Joseph because of the dreams. Even Jacob was miffed that young Joseph might think he would someday rule over him. His brothers already despised him because he was favored by Jacob; the dreams didn't help that situation at all.

Like his brothers, Joseph worked tending his father's sheep. One day, in a fit of jealousy, Joseph's brothers captured him when he came looking for them out in the fields. Initially, they plotted to kill him. But Reuben spoke up, uncomfortable with the idea of killing their own brother. He thought they should throw him into a cistern for the time being. So they did. As the brothers brooded over what to do next with their little dreamer of a brother, Judah said they shouldn't kill him but sell him to some Ishmaelite traders they saw coming down the road. (They were close to a roadway popular with caravans and traders that went from south Arabia to Giza.) And that's exactly what they did! They sold him for twenty pieces of silver. When the brothers returned to their father, Jacob, they made up a story, telling him that Joseph was killed by a lion.

The brothers showed Jacob Joseph's colorful coat ripped to shreds and drenched in blood. But it was all a lie. They had covered the coat in animal's blood to make it look like Joseph had been attacked and ripped to pieces. Believing Joseph was dead, Jacob mourned the loss of his beloved son.

The traders took Joseph to Egypt, where they sold him to Potiphar, the captain of Pharaoh's guard. Joseph, however, thrived in this new world. Over time, Potiphar recognized that God's hand was strong in Joseph's life and that Joseph was trustworthy, so he put him in charge of his entire household. Everything that Joseph did in command of Potiphar's house succeeded.

The Bible tells us that Joseph was good-looking and strong, and Potiphar's wife noticed. She made several advances on the young servant, but Joseph refused her each time. Finally, one day she approached Joseph and asked him to sleep with her; she clung to his cloak. But again Joseph refused, and this time he left her holding his cloak and ran off. He literally ran out of his cloak!

Spurned, Potiphar's wife made up a lie. She told her husband that Joseph tried to rape her. So Potiphar imprisoned Joseph.

First he's thrown into a cistern and sold as a slave by his brothers, and then he finds some success in Potiphar's house, only to be wrongly accused by Potiphar's wife.

Now Joseph's unjustly imprisoned.

He can't catch a break.

In prison, he accurately interpreted two dreams of his fellow inmates, who happened to be Pharaoh's former cupbearer and baker. The cupbearer dreamed of a vine with three branches with ripened clusters that turned into grapes. He squeezed the grapes into Pharaoh's cup. The baker dreamed of three baskets of bread on his head. In the top basket there were baked goods for Pharaoh, but the birds were eating them out of the basket.

Joseph offered to interpret the dreams. To the cupbearer, he said the dream meant the cupbearer would be restored to his former position. Joseph told the cupbearer to remember him afterward and that he'd done nothing to deserve prison. To the baker, he said the dream meant that Pharaoh would impale the baker and that the birds would eat his flesh.

Can you guess which fellow prisoner was set free and which was killed by Pharaoh? That's right. Joseph got the dreams right, and the cupbearer was set free, but he did not remember Joseph. Meanwhile Joseph found favor with the jailer and was put in charge of all the prisoners. Though Joseph was mistreated at every turn, he yet retained favor with God.

When Pharaoh was troubled by his dreams and needed a dream interpreted, the cupbearer finally remembered Joseph and his ability to interpret dreams, and Joseph was brought before Pharaoh. Joseph predicted seven years of plentiful harvest and seven years of famine. Like Potiphar and the jailer before him, Pharaoh noticed something special about Joseph and promoted him, placing him in charge of his kingdom.

Joseph became the most trusted and highest-ranking official in all of Egypt—Pharaoh's second-in-command. And just as he predicted, a great famine came to the whole region, including Canaan, where his father, Jacob, and his entire family lived. People came to Egypt from all over, seeking food and provisions.

A REUNION AND A CHANCE
FOR VENGEANCE

The epic story of Joseph ushers in one of the most crucial times of biblical history. To get to the very well-known place in history where the Israelites find themselves enslaved by the Egyptians, you first have to learn how they got to Egypt. Well, here's how.

One day during the famine, Joseph's brothers came to Egypt, seeking help. Joseph was the governor, the one in charge of distributing the grain to people who came to buy it. Little did they know, their little brother was now the official standing before them. Joseph realized they didn't recognize him, so he tested them. He spoke harshly with them and accused them of spying. But the brothers pleaded their case.

"Tell me about your family. Is your father alive?"

"Your servants were twelve brothers," they replied, "the sons of one man, who lives in the land of Canaan. The youngest is now with our father, and one is no more" (Gen. 42:13).

Through Joseph's questioning, he discovered that the brothers had left the youngest sibling, Benjamin, at home with their father. Joseph told them that before they could return home, they would have to send for their younger brother to prove their story. So Joseph imprisoned all the brothers for a few days. While in prison, the brothers thought over Joseph's request.

After a few days in jail, Joseph came to them and said, "Do this and you will live, for I fear God: If you are honest men, let one of your brothers stay here in prison, while the rest of you go and take grain back for your starving households. But you must bring your youngest brother to me, so that your words may be verified and that you may not die" (vv. 18–20).

And so the brothers made ready to do so.

As they were standing there, they talked to one another in their own language.

"Surely we are being punished because of our brother," one of them said. "We saw how distressed he was when he pleaded with us for his life, but we would not listen; that's why this distress has come on us" (v. 21).

"Didn't I tell you not to sin against the boy?" replied Reuben. "But you wouldn't listen! Now we must give an accounting for his blood" (v. 22). They didn't know Joseph understood them, because he was pretending to use an interpreter.

Finally, leaving Simeon, the other nine brothers returned home with the bad news. Imagine for a moment the journey home, knowing they had to face their father. Jacob couldn't believe it. Not only had he lost Joseph years ago, but now Simeon was captured, and the governor wanted Benjamin too. Grieved, Jacob refused to let his sons take Benjamin. He would not give up another son, although he realized that in so doing, he was essentially giving up Simeon. It was a lose-lose situation. But Benjamin was the blood brother of Joseph; both were from Jacob's beloved Rachel. He would not, for anything, give him up.

Then Judah spoke up. "Father, I will bear the full weight of responsibility for Benjamin's safety," he promised Jacob. But how could Jacob believe him? Hadn't Joseph also been in his care—in all their care!—before? But finally, Jacob relented and sent Benjamin along with his brothers back to Egypt.

The brothers returned to Egypt with Benjamin. Joseph's messenger greeted them and invited them to Joseph's home. Fearing for their lives, the brothers accepted the invitation and attended lunch at Joseph's house.

"Why would he ask us to his home?" they wondered.

As they sat at the table, Joseph noticed that their youngest brother, Benjamin, had made the trip. Keep in mind, Joseph and Benjamin were the two youngest brothers, and their mother was the woman Jacob truly loved, Rachel. The sight of his brother overwhelmed Joseph with emotion and forced him to leave the table. He exited the dining room and entered a private room, where he wept. When he returned to the table, Joseph asked for the food to be served. The servers gave Benjamin five times the serving his brothers received, a great honor to the youngest sibling. So they all ate and drank freely.

Can you see the revelry? They thought the worst, but now the situation had turned. They relaxed and perhaps breathed a collective sigh of relief. But was it too good to be true?

Following the meal, Joseph held up his end of the bargain and gave the brothers as much grain as their donkeys could carry. But he asked his servant to plant his own silver cup in Benjamin's grain bag, along with the silver he brought to pay for his grain. The brothers hadn't gone far down the road when Joseph's steward ran out to them.

"What have you done?" said the steward. "Why have you repaid good with evil, stealing my master's own silver cup?"

The brothers were astonished at the accusation and pled with Joseph's steward.

"We did not do this. But if one of us did, that brother will die and we will become your servants."

Joseph's steward replied, "Whoever possesses the cup in their bag will become a slave to Joseph, and the rest will be sent home."

The brothers agreed.

They dropped their bags of grain and opened them.

When Benjamin opened his bag, Joseph's silver cup was revealed. The brothers ripped their clothes and cried out in anguish.

"How could this happen?" they asked.

Since they had returned to Egypt for food, the brothers could not catch a break. They were walking Joseph's path now, directed by Joseph himself. They knew they couldn't lose another brother. Their aging father, Jacob, would be crushed to the point of death.

When the brothers returned to Joseph, they threw themselves at his mercy. Judah, who had promised Jacob that he would take care of Benjamin and assured his father that he'd bring Benjamin home, pled with Joseph.

"If we return home without our youngest brother, our father will die. I cannot let that happen. Take me instead."

When Joseph heard that Judah was willing to sacrifice himself for the life of his brother and father, he was again struck with emotion.

"Leave us!" he cried out to all his servants.

The room, empty and quiet, brimmed with the passion of the brothers. The excruciating possibility of losing Benjamin was weighing heavily on all the brothers and was the push Judah needed to step toward sacrificing himself in order that his younger brother might live. The years, the pain—all had come full circle, and Joseph saw in front of him his brothers who finally loved each other, who were willing to die for one another.

Joseph wept in the presence of his brothers, so loudly that the servants heard him, and word got back to Pharaoh about how hard he cried.

"I am Joseph!" he exclaimed, finally revealing himself.

His brothers were shocked and terrified. They had believed he was dead all these years. They had anguished over the thought of losing another brother, and now this? Joseph was alive? How could this be?

The brothers feared for their lives and threw themselves at Joseph's feet. But Joseph eased their fears.

Joseph spoke kindly to them, and he embraced Benjamin and wept. He embraced all of his brothers, and they visited for some time. Joseph invited them to take some carts from Egypt and return with their father,

Jacob. So the brothers went home and told their father the news. Stunned and overwhelmed, Jacob couldn't believe it. And yet when he heard all that had happened, and that Joseph was alive, Jacob's spirit revived, for he had regained Simeon, Benjamin was free, and his once-dead son was alive! He and his entire household of more than sixty people returned with the brothers to Egypt.

Years later, after Jacob died in Egypt, Joseph's brothers once again were afraid. They were concerned that with their father's death, Joseph would now get his revenge. Joseph again had to calm their fears.

"Don't be afraid," he said to them. "Am I in the place of God? You intended to harm me, but God intended it for good to accomplish what is now being done, the saving of many lives. So then, don't be afraid. I will provide for you and your children" (Gen. 50:19–21).

––––––––––

Joseph's story grips readers with emotion as the brothers are reunited and their evil deeds are forgiven. Like the story of Mephibosheth, Joseph's story works as a story within the biblical story. Just as Mephibosheth goes from abandonment to being favored by the king, so Joseph goes from betrayal to being chosen by Pharaoh. It is another story of redemption. But that's not what I want to highlight right now. Instead let's allow Joseph's story to give us some context and set the stage for one of the Bible's most famous characters: Moses, the second character in our timeline.

The story of the Bible now begins to focus on the blessing God has promised and how it will take shape. And just as we've seen so far in the story, beauty usually comes through ashes.

SIX

GOD'S RESCUE PLAN: PART 2

The book of Genesis ends with Joseph's father, Jacob, and his brothers, at Pharaoh's request, moving their families to Egypt. Pharaoh lets them settle in the land of Goshen, which is located in the southeastern section of the Egyptian Nile Delta.

The Bible says, "Now the Israelites [whom we now know as the family of Jacob, descended from Isaac and Abraham] settled in Egypt in the region of Goshen. They acquired property there and were fruitful and increased greatly in number" (Gen. 47:27).

The settlement of the Israelites in Egypt began a time of occupation in that land that would last for more than four hundred years. Does that time range ring a bell? It's the exact amount of time God mentioned in Abraham's dream. During that time, Jacob and Joseph died, and a new pharaoh, who knew nothing of Joseph and his family, rose to power. He saw that the Israelites had now grown into their own nation, right under his nose. A lot can happen in four hundred years.

He dealt shrewdly with them and subjugated them and enslaved them. But it gets worse. This pharaoh was no one to trifle with. He then commanded his people to throw every newborn male Israelite child into the Nile River. It was a horror of a decree. And there was a great infanticide.

This harsh oppression and evil intent of Pharaoh set the stage for a hero to rise up and save the people from the oppression they faced. This hero's name was Moses.

MOSES, AN IMPORTANT HERO

Before we get into Moses' story, let's look at the Bible as a whole and break down the importance of Moses and his influence throughout the biblical narrative.

The Bible mentions the name of Moses more than eight hundred times. He's mentioned in nineteen of the Old Testament books and twelve of the New Testament books. In the second book, Exodus, through the fifth book, Deuteronomy, Moses plays a prominent role. His death takes place at the end of Deuteronomy. Moses' story holds one of the keys to the biblical narrative.

Let's stop here and take a look at the first part of the Bible. The Bible often refers to its first five books as the Book of Moses, the Law of Moses, or the Book of the Law of Moses. These five books are also referred to as the Pentateuch because it is made up of five books. Another name for this collection of five books is the Torah, which means "the instructions," or "the law."

To make things simple, let's use the Torah as the name for the five books. Two of the books in the Torah, Leviticus and Deuteronomy, are primarily the instructions, or the law, that God gives to Moses at Mount Sinai. In the fifth book of the Bible, Deuteronomy, Moses repeats much of the law found in Leviticus to a new generation. These laws play an important role in the rest of the Bible, especially in the life of the nation of Israel. Throughout the rest of the Old Testament, there are many references to the Law of Moses. Even in the New Testament, we find the writers referring to the Law of Moses, and there is an effort to follow its instructions.

As you can see, Moses plays a primary role in the biblical narrative, so important that you've probably heard the story of Moses, or bits and pieces of it. Perhaps you've watched one of the many movies on his life. Do you remember the movie *The Ten Commandments*, in which the famous actor Charlton Heston played Moses? More recently, Christian Bale, famous for his role in the Batman movies, played Moses in a film called *Exodus*.

Let's get into the story of Moses. I want to highlight a very important event in his story that often gets lumped into Moses' narrative with little emphasis or explanation. This event is called Passover. But let's not get ahead of ourselves. His story begins during a time of great fear among the Israelites, and in the waters of the Nile.

AMONG THE REEDS

During the Egyptian infanticide, a young mother had a baby boy and knew that he was a beautiful child. She hid him for three months, but when it looked like the secret would get out, she tried to save her young son's life by placing him in a basket and setting him afloat in the Nile River. No one could see her, but the baby's sister watched from a distance as the basket floated down the river, finally resting in the reeds. Just like in a movie in which the person you least expect shows up, the daughter of Pharaoh saw the basket in the reeds and sent one of her servants to retrieve it.

The boy's sister approached Pharaoh's daughter and asked her if she wanted to find a nurse for the baby from among the Israelite women. Pharaoh's daughter agreed. The sister went and found their mother, and the boy's mother nursed him. When he grew old enough, the boy's mother returned him to Pharaoh's daughter, who named him Moses, which means "I drew him out of the water."

When Moses became a young man, he was walking out in the country where his people, the Israelites, lived and worked under the harsh oppression of the Egyptians. When he saw one of the Egyptian guards dealing violently with one of the Israelites, he intervened and killed the Egyptian. Even though Moses was now technically the son of Pharaoh, this was still a grave offense. The next day, Moses saw two Israelites fighting, and when he tried to intervene and encourage peace, one of the men said, "Who put you in charge? Are you going to kill me like you did the Egyptian?"

Word had gotten out. When Pharaoh heard what Moses had done, he sought to kill him, so Moses fled for his life to Midian. Midian was a land that lay to the east of the region of Egypt and was home to the Midianites. Moses found refuge in Midian and became the son-in-law to Jethro, the priest of Midian, who gave Moses the hand of his daughter Zipporah in marriage. It was in the wilderness of Midian that Moses became familiar with the desert and found occupation as a shepherd. He would shepherd for forty years.

THE BURNING BUSH

Of the many stories associated with Moses, the story of the burning bush remains a favorite. Many years passed, and still the Israelites struggled under the oppression of the Egyptians. One day, the angel of the LORD appeared to Moses. While Moses was tending Jethro's flocks on the far side of Mount Horeb, also known as the mountain of God, he came upon a bush that was caught up in flames of fire, and yet the bush itself did not burn up. Intrigued, Moses went in for a closer look.

When the angel of the LORD saw that Moses walked toward the bush, he called out to Moses from *within* the bush.

"Moses!" came the voice.

"Here I am," replied Moses.

"Don't come any closer. The ground you're standing on is holy ground. Take off your sandals."

Moses removed his sandals.

Then the angel of the LORD introduced himself through the voice that came out of the burning bush.

"I am the God of Abraham, the God of Isaac, and the God of Jacob."

Whoa. Moses knew exactly who this God was, and he hid his face because he was afraid to look at God.

It's here in this holy encounter that God called Moses to save the children of Israel from the oppressive hand of Pharaoh.

"I have indeed seen the misery of my people in Egypt," said God. "I have heard them crying out because of their slave drivers, and I am concerned about their suffering. So I have come down to rescue them from the hand of the

Egyptians and to bring them up out of that land into a good and spacious land, a land flowing with milk and honey—the home of the Canaanites, Hittites, Amorites, Perizzites, Hivites and Jebusites. And now the cry of the Israelites has reached me, and I have seen the way the Egyptians are oppressing them. So now, go. I am sending you to Pharaoh to bring my people the Israelites out of Egypt" (Ex. 3:7–10).

Of course, Moses reacted like we all would—he was overjoyed at the opportunity to do such a great thing for God. Right?

Not exactly.

Moses responded with uncertainty and doubt.

"Who am I that I should go to Pharaoh and bring the Israelites out of Egypt?" he replied (v. 11).

"I will be with you," said God. "And this will be the sign to you that it is I who have sent you: When you have brought the people out of Egypt, you will worship God on this mountain" (v. 12).

Moses still wasn't convinced. Again he stalled.

"Well, let's suppose I do this thing," he said, "and deliver this message to Pharaoh. If they ask me the name of the God who sent me, what should I tell them?"

God's answer to Moses left little doubt as to his identity. If you look at the words in Exodus 3:14–15, God answered Moses three times.

First God says, "I AM WHO I AM" (v. 14).

Then, "Tell them I AM has sent you."

Finally, he says, "Say to the Israelites, 'The LORD, the

God of your fathers—the God of Abraham, the God of Isaac and the God of Jacob—has sent me to you.' This is my name forever, the name you shall call me from generation to generation" (v. 15).

God then instructed Moses to meet with the elders of Israel and give them the message, and he assured Moses they would believe him. But Moses gave God excuse after excuse for why he wasn't the right person for the job. He even asked God to send someone else! God was not pleased with Moses' response. But he compromised and gave Moses his brother, Aaron, as Moses' mouthpiece to Pharaoh. God reminded Moses to take his staff so that he could perform the signs he would need to convince the elders and Pharaoh that his message came with the power of I AM.

THE PASSOVER LAMB

So Moses did what God asked him to do. He went to the elders of Israel and, with the help of Aaron, gave them God's message. The two of them convinced the elders and then went before Pharaoh with God's message. But it didn't go so well.

Pharaoh said, "Who is the LORD, and why should I obey him and let the Israelites go? I don't know the LORD, so the answer is no."

Each time Moses asked Pharaoh to let the LORD's people go, he refused. And each time he refused, God struck the people of Egypt with a plague. He struck them with ten plagues in all: turned water to blood; sent frogs, gnats, and flies; killed livestock; brought on boils, hail, locusts, and darkness.

"Wait, that's only nine," you say.

You're correct. The final plague was the death of every firstborn male.

So Moses said to Pharaoh, "This is what the LORD says: 'About midnight I will go throughout Egypt. Every firstborn son in Egypt will die, from the firstborn son of Pharaoh, who sits on the throne, to the firstborn son of the female slave, who is at her hand mill, and all the firstborn of the cattle as well. There will be loud wailing throughout Egypt—worse than there has ever been or ever will be again. But among the Israelites not a dog will bark at any person or animal.' Then you will know that the LORD makes a distinction between Egypt and Israel. All these officials of yours will come to me, bowing down before me and saying, 'Go, you and all the people who follow you!' After that I will leave" (Ex. 11:4–8).

Then Moses turned in anger and left Pharaoh.

But how would the angel of death not touch the firstborn males of the Israelites?

God instructed Moses and Aaron to tell the people to slaughter a small lamb and smear the blood of the lamb on the doorposts of their homes. Every home on which the blood of the lamb was smeared, the angel of death would pass over.

God said to them, "On that same night [when you slaughter the lamb] I will pass through Egypt and strike down every firstborn of both people and animals, and I will bring judgment on all the gods of Egypt. I am the LORD. The blood will be a sign for you on the houses where you are, and when I see the blood, I will pass over you. No destructive plague will touch you when I strike Egypt.

"This is a day you are to commemorate; for the generations to come you shall celebrate it as a festival to the LORD—a lasting ordinance" (Ex. 12:12–14).

Moses went and instructed the elders to select lambs and then to kill the Passover lamb. And all the people listened to the instructions from Moses and Aaron. Moses reminded them that this would be a lasting ordinance before the LORD and that in the future, when their children ask them why they celebrate it, they should tell them, "It is the sacrifice of the LORD's Passover, for he passed over the houses of the people of Israel in Egypt, when he struck the Egyptians but spared our houses" (Ex. 12:27 ESV). When the people heard this, they bowed their heads and worshiped.

A LASTING ORDINANCE

The story of Passover is prominent throughout the Bible.

In the books of Leviticus, Numbers, and Deuteronomy, the children of Israel are commanded to remember the Passover every year.

The LORD's Passover begins at twilight on the fourteenth day of the first month.

—LEVITICUS 23:5

"Have the Israelites celebrate the Passover at the appointed time. Celebrate it at the appointed time, at twilight on the fourteenth day of this month, in accordance with all its rules and regulations."

So Moses told the Israelites to celebrate the Passover, and they did so in the Desert of Sinai at twilight on the fourteenth day of the first month. The Israelites did everything just as the LORD commanded Moses.

—NUMBERS 9:2–5

Observe the month of Aviv and celebrate the Passover of the LORD your God, because in the month of Aviv he brought you out of Egypt by night.

—DEUTERONOMY 16:1

During a later period in the history of Israel, we're told, the Israelites had quit following God's instruction and forgotten his law. When the instructions that were given to Moses were found and read, they began to celebrate Passover again. "The king gave this order to all the people: 'Celebrate the Passover to the LORD your God, as it is written in this Book of the Covenant.' Neither in the days of the judges who led Israel nor in the days of the kings of Israel and the kings of Judah had any such Passover been observed. But in the eighteenth year of King Josiah, this Passover was celebrated to the LORD in Jerusalem" (2 Kings 23:21–23).

After a period of exile, when the children of Israel returned to their homeland, the Passover was reinstituted. "On the fourteenth day of the first month, the exiles celebrated the Passover. The priests and Levites had purified themselves and were all ceremonially clean. The Levites slaughtered the Passover lamb for all the exiles, for their relatives the priests and for themselves" (Ezra 6:19–20).

In the New Testament, other than the stories surrounding Jesus' birth, we find only one brief story of Jesus before he was an adult. In that story, we read that his parents traveled to Jerusalem every year for the Feast of the Passover (Luke 2:41). In the account, it says Jesus was twelve years old, and as his parents were returning home with a group of friends and family, they noticed Jesus was not with them. They had to return, only to find Jesus in the temple, having a discussion with the teachers.

We also read that during Jesus' adult life, he observed Passover. In the now-famous painting of Leonardo da Vinci titled *The Last Supper*, we see Jesus and his disciples celebrating Passover. The painting is called *The Last Supper* because this is the last meal Jesus would have with his disciples before his crucifixion. The Gospel of

Matthew records Jesus' celebration of Passover: "On the first day of the Festival of Unleavened Bread, the disciples came to Jesus and asked, 'Where do you want us to make preparations for you to eat the Passover?'

"He replied, 'Go into the city to a certain man and tell him, "The Teacher says: My appointed time is near. I am going to celebrate the Passover with my disciples at your house."' So the disciples did as Jesus had directed them and prepared the Passover" (Matt. 26:17–19).

But I'm getting ahead of myself. We'll get to Jesus soon enough. I just wanted to show you that what began that fateful night in Egypt carried on.

Passover is instituted in the second book of the Bible and is found throughout the Bible's story. The Passover, then, is one of the elements that ties the books of the Bible together. Even today, there are those of the Jewish faith who celebrate Passover, using this story from the Bible to inform their observance. I recently received an email from a Jewish rabbi friend, telling me of his dietary observance and the special food preparation he will be making during the upcoming Passover season.

Passover is the event God used to set his people free from slavery. It is the ultimate story within the story. Remember the story we recounted earlier about Mephibosheth? The story of Mephibosheth is a story that easily can be missed. But it tells a similar Exodus-type story. It tells of the rescue of Mephibosheth—from hiding in the desert to being placed in the king's house. In

Exodus, God rescued the children of Israel from slavery and sent them on their way to the promised land. One is a story easily missed, the other a focus in the rest of the Bible.

SEVEN

MYSTERIOUS MESSENGERS

The children of Israel are free! Well, at least from the oppression of Pharaoh. When they leave Egypt, the Egyptians are so ready for them to be gone that they give their clothes and jewelry and money to them as a way to say, "Good riddance!" So in effect, the Israelites plunder Egypt without raising a finger.

But Pharaoh goes back on his word and pursues Moses and the entire nation of Israel with his army because he intends to destroy them!

God has other plans.

When the children of Israel walk as far as the shore of the Red Sea, they begin to grumble among themselves. They even say crazy things like, "We were better off in Egypt. Now we will die out here in the desert!" But God instructs Moses to hold out his staff over the water. Moses obeys, and God rolls back the waters of the sea and creates a path the Israelites can walk on. They cross the Red Sea by walking right through it, on dry ground.

They reach the other side of the sea, but Pharaoh is still in pursuit. He doesn't even stop and think that perhaps the waters may fall back into the sea. Sure enough, they do, and all of Pharaoh's armies are destroyed. Thus ends the saga of the oppression of Israel at the hand of Pharaoh.

———

So far, in our journey through the story of the Bible, we've followed the sojourn of humanity in a world marred by sin and evil because of man's refusal to obey God. But time and time again, God shows up and provides a way to start over, or a path to salvation—like Israel getting freed from Egypt.

Several times in the narrative, we've come across a prediction of the future, like when God caused Abraham to fall asleep and foretold the four hundred years of slavery in Egypt (Gen. 15:12–22). This foretelling has a name. It's called prophecy, and it plays a major role in the biblical narrative. It's like a thread woven throughout the fabric of the story, connecting the stories within the story to the whole.

In this chapter, I want to take another break from the biblical narrative and look a little closer at this interesting practice of prediction called prophecy. Let's dive in.

WHAT IS PROPHECY?

Every year, people make predictions. They predict who will win elections, who will win the Super Bowl, and who will win the World Series, and in March every year during March Madness, they predict who will win the NCAA basketball tournament. Every year the *Farmers' Almanac* predicts what the weather will be like for the following year.

There are those who claim to be able to predict the future, such as astrologers and fortune-tellers, and of course there is a prediction in your fortune cookie at the local Chinese restaurant. One who is well known for predicting the future is Michel de Nostredame, better known as Nostradamus. He wrote a book in 1555 titled *Les Prophéties* ("The Prophecies"), in which he claimed to predict future world events.

The Bible also contains predictions, or prophecies. They are spoken by the prophets. Some of the prophecies have their fulfillment chronicled in the biblical records, and some of the Bible claims point to the future. One of the reasons it's important to take a look at the Bible's prophecies is to see how they connect, how predictions given in earlier books connect to stories told in later books. But there's another reason to look closely at what the prophets say.

Besides the prophecies, prophets also gave instructions or admonitions. They acted as God's messengers to his people. Moses is an example. When Moses went up to Mount Sinai, he was given the Ten Commandments and other instructions to give to the people of Israel. These were ethical guidelines for the entire nation. Sometimes a prophet arrived on the scene to tell the people that God was not happy with their behavior and that they needed to stop disobeying him. So while prophets did prophesy, they also delivered God's messages to his people.

PROPHECY AND PROPHETS

We find the very first example of prophecy in the Bible in Genesis 3. This particular prophecy foretells future events.

> "I will put enmity
>   between you and the woman,
>   and between your offspring and hers;
>   he will crush your head,
>   and you will strike his heel."
>   —GENESIS 3:15

In this cryptic verse, God himself speaks. He predicts how the disobedient acts of Adam and Eve will affect the future. He speaks these words to the serpent. Notice the prophetic nature of God's words. He's speaking of the offspring of Eve, and the relationship they will have with the serpent. He says the offspring of Eve will crush the head of the serpent and that the serpent will strike the heel of Eve's offspring. It sounds very strange, but these words predict that something is going to happen in the future.

We run into our first prophet in the Torah. In the book of Genesis, God refers to Abraham as a prophet (Gen. 20:7). The Bible names 133 prophets, which includes 16 women. In the New Testament book of Ephesians, the apostle Paul declares that God's church is made up of prophets and apostles (Eph. 2:19–20).

What are prophets like? What makes them unique?

A good example of a prophet known for his unique actions is Ezekiel. His story is written in the first person, and we're immediately caught up in an otherworldly scene with some of the most bizarre visuals in all of the Bible—outside of the book of Revelation, which also happens to be a book written of future events.

Throughout the book of Ezekiel, we find this prophet of God doing some unorthodox things, like lying on his side for 395 days, which signified Israel's 395 years of rebellion against God. Crazy acts like this were used by the prophets as signals to their audience. They helped communicate God's message.

Ezekiel was one of the people of Israel. He came from a family of priests. He starts his book by simply giving us the time of year, the name of the current king of Israel, how long the king and the people have been held captive by the Babylonians (five years), and the fact that the vision came to him while he was living among the captives at the Kebar River near Babylon.

Ezekiel takes us on an incredible ride as he watches a cloud of lightning approach him from the north. We meet four four-headed, four-winged angelic beings who stand beneath a vast expanse. Each angelic creature has the head of a man, lion, eagle, and ox. When they move, two of their wings point up to the expanse and the majestic throne on which God sits. From the waist up, this likeness of God looks like burning metal, and from the waist down, he looks like flames of fire.

Ezekiel goes into great detail about this initial scene, in which he comes face-to-face with the likeness of the glory of God. After he describes the scene, we discover what it is that God wants Ezekiel to do and the message God wants to send to his people, the children of Israel.

What is that message?

Ezekiel tells the people of Israel that God will judge them for being rebellious. It seems like such harsh news for people who are already being held captive in a foreign land. But then Ezekiel gives them hope. He points to a future leader, a new king—a king like their beloved King David, the same David we read about in the chapter about Mephibosheth (Ezek. 34:23–24). So Ezekiel brings a message of justice (God's judgment) and a message of hope (a future king).

Ezekiel was known as a prophet of God. Prophets had strange messages of plain truth for the people of God. They warned, they encouraged, they said what was going to happen. Their lives and messages connect many of the Bible stories, in shocking and compassionate ways.

FALSE PROPHETS

Prophets weren't always treated very well by the people they were trying to help. At times, the people didn't like what they had to say. When the prophet's message was that the people had to change their ways, often the prophet was attacked. They also came against *false* prophets. False prophets acted as foils to the prophets. They told the people of Israel a false story and contradicted the message of God told by the true prophets.

Unlike a real prophet, false prophets did not stand in the presence of God or receive a message from God himself. Rather they used their own dreams and threats to turn God's people away from him.

In the book of Jeremiah, we find a classic example of what false prophets did and how God feels about them.

This is what the LORD Almighty says:

> "Do not listen to what the prophets are prophesying
> to you;
> they fill you with false hopes.
> They speak visions from their own minds,
> not from the mouth of the LORD.
> They keep saying to those who despise me,
> 'The LORD says: You will have peace.'
> And to all who follow the stubbornness of their
> hearts
> they say, 'No harm will come to you.'
> But which of them has stood in the council of the
> LORD
> to see or to hear his word?
> Who has listened and heard his word? . . .
> I did not send these prophets,
> yet they have run with their message;
> I did not speak to them,
> yet they have prophesied."
> —JEREMIAH 23:16–18, 21

God takes false prophecy seriously.

God issued a harsh warning to anybody who claimed to be speaking for him but hadn't heard from him. Right after Moses told the people that another prophet would come, he gave this warning from God: "A prophet who presumes to speak in my name anything I have not commanded, or a prophet who speaks in the name of other gods, is to be put to death" (Deut. 18:20).

Now, those are strong words from God. Then he immediately tells the people how to determine whether a prophet is a true prophet. "You may say to yourselves, 'How can we know when a message has not been spoken by the LORD?' If what a prophet proclaims in the name of the LORD does not take place or come true, that is a message the LORD has not spoken. That prophet has spoken presumptuously, so do not be alarmed" (vv. 21–22). And yet even in the face of such dire consequences, false prophets persisted in contradicting God.

THE STORY OF CAPTIVITY

A specific example of false prophecies given by false prophets is when the Israelites were being punished and were being taken captive to Babylon. The false prophets were distributing lies. They told the Israelites that the captivity was only a blip on the radar and that they would be right back to their homeland. And since they'd return home soon, the false prophets told the people not to serve the king of Babylon.

But this message gave false hopes to the Israelites, and it is not at all what God had said. God said, "Do not listen to what the prophets are prophesying to you; they fill you with false hopes. They speak visions from their own minds, not from the mouth of the LORD. . . . So do not listen to your prophets, your diviners, your interpreters of dreams, your mediums or your sorcerers who tell you, 'You will not serve the king of Babylon'" (Jer. 23:16; 27:9). The prophecy that God had given to Jeremiah was that the Israelites were going to be captive in Babylon for seventy years. It is mentioned in two other books: 2 Chronicles and Daniel.[3]

So the false prophets were saying something different than what God had said.[4] In the story of the Israelites' captivity, these false prophets created tension in the narrative. Would the people listen to God, or would they heed the words of the false prophets?

This builds intrigue. I want to know what's going to happen. Why is Jeremiah's message from God so important in the grand scheme of things—so important that God issues such dire consequences for people who contradict the message?

JEREMIAH'S MESSAGE

Let's back up and take a look at the situation that Jeremiah was talking about, because it was predicted many years before and because it connects to one of the major narrative threads woven throughout the entire Bible.

To start, let's look at the biblical timeline after the Torah. Remember, "the Torah" is just another way to refer to the first five books of the Bible.

At the end of the Torah, the Israelites were ready to enter the land God had promised to Abraham. Moses had passed away, and Joshua was appointed to take over the leadership of Israel. The time period from when the Israelites take the land to when the first king is established is referred to as the period of the judges.

What's a judge?

Judges were "leaders Israel had from the time of the elders who outlived Joshua until the time of the monarchy."[5] They were established by God to save Israel from outside enemies. Here's how the book of Judges defines their role. "Then the LORD raised up judges, who saved them out of the hands of these raiders" (Judg. 2:16). This was a time when there was no formal king appointed to rule Israel, but judges ruled the people. The Bible describes the condition of the people as the judges' period ends: it says everybody did what was right in their own eyes (Judg. 21:25). This was not a good time.

The period of the judges ended as the people asked for a king like all the other nations had. God granted the people their request; a king was asked for, and a king was given.

During the reign of three kings—Saul, David, and Solomon—the kingdom stayed together. After Solomon's reign, the kingdom split in two. The Northern Kingdom kept the name Israel, while the Southern Kingdom took the name Judah. This period is referred to as the divided kingdom of Israel.

For a time, both kingdoms continued with their own kings, until both kingdoms were taken captive by other kingdoms. Israel was first taken into captivity by the Assyrians; Judah was later captured by the Babylonians.

I like looking at timelines; it helps me place the stories in context.

In the biblical timeline, we find that the period of the judges begins around 1350 BC and ends sometime before 1050 BC.

The united kingdom of Israel existed until the end of Solomon's reign, sometime after 950 BC. Then the kingdom of Israel divided after Solomon's death. The age of the two kingdoms ended in 722 BC for Israel and 586 BC for Judah. Here's the visual.

Judges	1350–1050 BC
United kingdom (Israel)	1050–950 BC
Divided kingdom (Israel & Judah)	950–722 BC & 586 BC
Captivity	586–516 BC
Return	516–400 BC

At the end of the Old Testament, the children of Israel returned to what had become their homeland. According to the Bible, the return from captivity was seventy years after they were taken captive. The Old Testament writings end around 400 BC.

Throughout the story of the Israelite people, we find the writings of the prophets, those who claimed to be speaking for God, warning the people as they forgot their LORD. The period of captivity was not a surprise, because it had been prophesied by Moses and warned of by the prophets. In the book of Leviticus, one of the five books of the Torah, God gives a warning to the Israelites, that if they do not follow his instructions, they will be punished. Eventually, the punishment will end in them being scattered. God says, "I will scatter you among the nations and will draw out my sword and pursue you. Your land will be laid waste, and your cities will lie in ruins" (Lev. 26:33). Deuteronomy, the last book of the Torah, says the same thing.[6] Toward the end of Deuteronomy, it gets even more specific. It says that they will have a king and have to serve under another king (Deut. 28:36).

Now, keep in mind that in the biblical timeline, the law was given to Moses approximately seven hundred to eight hundred years *before* Israel and Judah were taken captive. The warning of captivity was repeated to the Israelites by the prophets on several occasions.

Our good friend Ezekiel specifically ties the warning of Moses to the captivity when he quotes God as saying, "With uplifted hand I swore to them in the wilderness that I would disperse them among the nations and scatter them through the countries" (Ezek. 20:23). Nehemiah, writing after the captivity, reminds the Israelites of God's warning through Moses when he says in his prayer to God, "Remember the instruction you gave your servant Moses, saying, 'If you are unfaithful, I will scatter you among the nations" (Neh. 1:8).[7]

It's interesting to see how the messages of prophecy weave events together.

God warns Moses of a future captivity.

The prophets warn that because of the Israelites' disobedience, they will be overtaken and held in captivity in foreign lands.

The children of Israel are taken captive.

Later on, after they return from their captivity, Nehemiah reminds the people of God's warning and how it came to pass, just as God promised.

MESSAGES OF HOPE

Not only did God give Moses the commandments and also warn him of the coming captivity; God also gave him a message of hope to give the people of Israel. Moses prophesied about the coming of another prophet—one like him, only greater. We find it in the book of Deuteronomy.

The LORD your God will raise up for you a prophet like me from among you, from your fellow Israelites. You must listen to him. For this is what you asked of the LORD your God at Horeb on the day of the assembly when you said, "Let us not hear the voice of the LORD our God nor see this great fire anymore, or we will die."

The LORD said to me: "What they say is good. I will raise up for them a prophet like you from among their fellow Israelites, and I will put my words in his mouth. He will tell them everything I command him. I myself will call to account anyone who does not listen to my words that the prophet speaks in my name."

—DEUTERONOMY 18:15–19

Another prophet is coming. Who will it be? The prophecy alone is enough to enliven hope within a person, especially a person who has lived through captivity or trial or hardship, like the people of Israel have. Abraham was promised that through him all the people of the earth would be blessed, and now Moses tells of a future prophet like him. In the Prophets, along with the instructions, the predictions, and the warnings of judgment for disobedience, there is this thread of hope that continues to show up.

———

Once the beginning of the Bible's story is told in the Torah, the rest of the Old Testament focuses on the story of God dealing with the nation of Israel. They are given instructions to live by and warnings that if they disobey, there will be consequences. It tells of their victories and downfalls. The prophecies in the Torah that predict the captivity of the nations of Israel and Judah connect the whole of the Old Testament.

EIGHT

THE TIME OF KINGS

It's been a wild ride.

From humanity's choice to live for self rather than remain in communion with God (that sin problem), to God flooding the earth and starting over with Noah's family, to God finally picking Abraham's family as the means to bring blessing and reunion to humanity once again. It has been a ride.

When we left off, the Israelites had found themselves on the other side of the Red Sea, freed from the oppression of Pharaoh and the Egyptians. God had told them that he would lead them to the promised land, a territory called Canaan. It was where Jacob and his twelve sons, including

Joseph, lived before moving to Egypt during the famine. The promised land was a land "flowing with milk and honey" (Ex. 3:8), a land that was beautiful and covered with hills and pastures and filled with honey from the bees living there. But their journey, which should have taken only about two weeks, ended up lasting forty years.

The Israelites pitched camp at Mount Sinai when God summoned Moses to the mountain. Moses climbed to the top and waited for six days before he encountered the presence of God. Finally, God showed up and Moses met with him for forty days. During that time, God gave Moses a set of rules to live by. You and I know the cornerstone of these rules as the Ten Commandments.

THE TEN COMMANDMENTS

1. Do not have any other god before God.
2. Do not make yourself an idol.
3. Do not take the Lord's name in vain.
4. Remember the Sabbath Day and keep it holy.
5. Honor your mother and father.
6. Do not murder.
7. Do not commit adultery.
8. Do not steal.
9. Do not testify or bear false witness against your neighbor.
10. Do not covet.[8]

When Moses returned from the top of Mount Sinai with these new rules, he found the people engaged in idol worship. They feared something had happened to Moses, so they made a god for themselves out of gold. Moses was furious.

During this time, God instructed Moses on how to build a tabernacle. Remember that in our discussion of God's holiness? This was a portable place that contained the presence of God. Through Moses, God told the Israelites how to order their camp and how to worship him and how to travel together as a nation, with God's presence at the center of it. So they were basically a nation of God's people, and he was their King, living among them.

And what about this land God had promised to Israel? Well, Moses sent twelve spies to assess the land of Canaan, each a chieftain from one of the tribes of Israel. But when the spies returned, they gave Moses a grim report. Except for Caleb and Joshua. Yes, the land was just as God said it was. "It does flow with milk and honey!" (Num. 13:27) was the report, and the spies even returned with some of the fruit as proof. "But the people look like giants," said ten of them, "and the cities are massive and well fortified." Only Caleb and Joshua believed God would give them the land.

Because of their disbelief, God punished Israel, and they had to wander for forty years in the desert. No man from that generation—including the great Moses—would enter the promised land, except Caleb and Joshua.

A KINGDOM OF OUR OWN

As mentioned, Moses died at the end of the book of Deuteronomy, the final book of the Torah. Joshua took over. Through Joshua's leadership, Israel took the land, but they failed to drive out all the nations living in it, which God had commanded them to do. As a result, they continued to fight with these nations for years. God also told them not to worship the false gods of these people. But Israel disobeyed time and time again. During this time, God appointed judges, leaders to guide Israel. Israel would fall into idol worship, their enemies would begin to oppress them, causing Israel to cry out to God for help, and then God would send them a leader. A judge.

Eventually, Israel cried out for a king of their own.

"We want a king like every other nation has," they said.

The people went to the prophet Samuel and asked him to ask God for a king. Samuel didn't like the idea, but God told Samuel it was okay. "The people have not rejected you, Samuel," said God. "They have rejected me."

At God's direction, Samuel appointed Saul to be king over Israel. Saul was from the tribe of Benjamin. He was a tall man and impressive to look at. But Saul didn't last long on the throne before he disobeyed God. When God instructed him to destroy the Amalekites and all their possessions, Saul let Agag, the king, and the best of their livestock live. As a result of Saul's disobedience, God removed his blessing from Saul and told Samuel to anoint a shepherd boy from the tribe of Judah, a young man named David, one of our main characters.

If you remember, back when Joseph's brothers discovered that they would lose their brother Benjamin, it was Judah who stood before Joseph and offered himself instead. "Take me," he told Joseph. The Bible tells us that David was a descendant of Judah.

When one thinks of all the characters in the Bible, both the Old Testament and the New, David springs to mind.

As a young shepherd, he defeats the Philistine's mighty champion, Goliath, with nothing more than a sling and some rocks. He goes on to have other victories over Israel's enemies. As David's military triumphs multiply, his renown grows, and this causes King Saul to resent him.

He's hired to play his lyre (a stringed instrument) for Saul when the king's spirit is troubled. Circumstances bring him closer to the king, who becomes increasingly jealous of David.

Saul's jealousy rises so much that he schemes to kill David. He seeks to take advantage of his daughter's love for David and offers Michal to him as his wife. The bride price? David must provide one hundred Philistine foreskins; then Michal is David's. But the plan backfires when David succeeds in the task and even doubles the amount: he kills two hundred Philistines and gives their foreskins to King Saul.

David eventually has to go on the run as Saul's efforts

to kill him continue. Eventually, Saul is killed in battle, opening the door for David.

David becomes king over all of Israel. God calls David "a man after his own heart" (1 Sam. 13:14), and though David has his failures, his renown and his bloodline remain significant. In the book of the Bible about his kingship, we find this passage known as the Davidic Covenant. It is God's promises specifically to David. Here is what God tells the prophet Nathan.

"Now then, tell my servant David, 'This is what the LORD Almighty says: I took you from the pasture, from tending the flock, and appointed you ruler over my people Israel. I have been with you wherever you have gone, and I have cut off all your enemies from before you. Now I will make your name great, like the names of the greatest men on earth. And I will provide a place for my people Israel and will plant them so that they can have a home of their own and no longer be disturbed. Wicked people will not oppress them anymore, as they did at the beginning and have done ever since the time I appointed leaders over my people Israel. I will also give you rest from all your enemies.

"'The LORD declares to you that the LORD himself will establish a house for you: When your days are over and you rest with your ancestors, I will raise up your offspring to succeed you, your own flesh and blood, and I will establish his kingdom. He is the one who will build a house for my Name, and I will establish the throne of his kingdom forever. I will be his father, and he will be my son. When he does wrong, I will punish him with a rod wielded by men, with floggings inflicted by human hands. But my love will never be taken away from him, as I took it away from Saul, whom I removed from before you. Your house and your kingdom will endure forever before me; your throne will be established forever.'"

—2 SAMUEL 7:8–16

The final sentence here looks like it doesn't belong. Why? Because it sounds like God is talking about someone who is not a king in the way that David is presently king. How can anyone's throne be established forever? Still, this is God's promise to David. But when we look at David's kingdom, we find that it does not look like a kingdom that lasts forever. Which leaves us to wonder whose kingdom God means.

During his reign, David's failures are exposed. At the height of his power, he decides not to go to war with his troops—being a great warrior was a distinguishing factor of David—and instead he stays home. During his idle time, when he is up on his roof walking, he spies a lovely woman, Bathsheba, taking a bath. He watches her bathe and desires her. He has Bathsheba brought to his chamber. But she is married to Uriah, one of David's great soldiers. David gives in to his lust.

He sleeps with Bathsheba and she becomes pregnant. Now he is in a mess. To cover up his affair, David sends for Uriah and gives him some time off from fighting and encourages him to go and be with his wife, hoping that he will lay with her. But Uriah has too much honor. He will not sleep with his wife while the men are out fighting. David's initial plan fails.

He then tries to get Uriah drunk so that he will go sleep with his wife. But Uriah, when it comes time for sleep, stays with the servants.

Finally, David, desperate to cover his tracks, sends a note with Uriah to Joab, David's general and commanding officer. He instructs Joab to send Uriah to the front lines, where the fighting is fiercest, and then withdraw from Uriah so that he will be killed.

The deed does not go unnoticed by God. Nathan, God's prophet, confronts David about his rebellious acts and tells him he will lose the son born to Bathsheba and that calamity will come upon him from his own family.

David's son Absalom becomes part of that calamity when he comes of age and revolts, turning Israel against David. In the uprising, more than twenty thousand men die, with David's men routing the troops from Israel. As Absalom is riding his donkey in the forest, his hair gets caught in an oak tree. David's commander, Joab, gets word and rushes to the sight. Before the fighting began, David gave strict instructions that Absalom was not to be injured. But Joab disregards the order and plunges three javelins into Absalom's heart. Joab's armor-bearers finish the job. That day, even though David's men are victorious, David mourns for his son.

"O Absalom, my son, my son!" he said over and over (2 Sam. 19:4), his heart heavy with grief, his life piling up the calamity Nathan promised.

But David's second son with Bathsheba, the woman he had the affair with, becomes the third king of Israel. His name is Solomon.

Solomon makes a name for himself as one of the wisest humans to ever live. Much of the book of Proverbs, found in the Old Testament, is attributed to him, as are Song of Songs and Ecclesiastes. Solomon also builds a temple for God—something David desired to do, but God told him that it was not for him to do; his son would do it.

After the reign of Solomon, which lasts until about 931 BC, the kingdom of Israel divides. Why? For the same reason many revolts take place: the government's "heavy yoke" (1 Kings 12:4).

Upon Solomon's death, his son Rehoboam is made king. The people come to him and ask him to lighten the load put on them by his father because of Solomon's building projects. After consulting with both his older and his younger advisors, Rehoboam takes the advice of the younger ones. He tells the people, "My father made your yoke heavy; I will make it even heavier" (v. 14). So the people revolt. The result is a division of the nation.

The Southern Kingdom remains true to Solomon's son,

Rehoboam, and is composed of two tribes, the tribe of Benjamin and the tribe of Judah. The Southern Kingdom takes the name Judah, and their capital is Jerusalem.

The other ten tribes of Israel, the Northern Kingdom, follow Jeroboam, who was an official to Solomon. They take the name Israel, and Samaria is their capital. The Northern Kingdom, Israel, falls into idol worship. But they aren't alone. The rulers from both kingdoms fall into idolatry and disobedience. During this time, prophets like Elijah, Elisha, Isaiah, and Jeremiah rise to prominence as voices for God to warn the people of both nations about their disobedience. At the same time, these prophets are pointing forward—to a day when a future king will arise and bring restoration and redemption to Israel.

Both kingdoms weaken spiritually and militarily, and eventually the Northern Kingdom, Israel, falls to Assyria, in 722 BC. The Southern Kingdom, Judah, has some good leaders. They do not fall until 136 years later, when Nebuchadnezzar, Babylon's king, destroys Jerusalem in 586 BC. The fall of these two nations raises the question of how God's promises will come true. How will David's throne endure forever? And what about Abraham's descendants blessing all nations? And a prophet like Moses who is to come?

This is the mess left after the time of the kings and the divided kingdom of Israel. What happens next is unexpected, to say the least.

NINE

ON WISDOM AND POETRY

But hold on.

Before we take the next step into the unexpected, we need to address what is perhaps the most beautiful portion of the Bible: the books of poetry and wisdom.

They are Psalms, Proverbs, Song of Songs, Job, and Ecclesiastes. Each of these books has an interesting story of its own, and at first glance, how they fit into the overall narrative might not be so obvious. On the other hand, they represent some of the most beloved stories and writings in the Bible. Let's look at three books from this section, starting with Psalms.

THE BOOK OF PSALMS

The popular website Bible Gateway composed a list of the top ten most read books of the Bible, and two of the poetic and wisdom books made the top ten.[9] Can you guess what number one was?

Psalms.

You might open a Bible—say, at a hotel—and turn to the middle. There you'd most likely discover the book of Psalms. This is the longest book in the Bible and is composed of Hebrew poetry, much of which is attributed to King David himself, although there are a few other contributors. Some might ask, why a book of poetry? And what place does it have in the story of the Bible?

Psalms is often called a book of lament, or complaining. The psalms detail the sufferings and complaints of mankind, and within that suffering there's comfort.

Even people unfamiliar with the rest of the Bible or its story may recognize Psalm 23. It's become a familiar text, like the Lord's Prayer. It speaks of God being a guide and comforter through life's ups and downs.

> The LORD is my shepherd, I lack nothing.
>   He makes me lie down in green pastures,
>   he leads me beside quiet waters,
>   he refreshes my soul.
> He guides me along the right paths
>   for his name's sake.

Even though I walk
　　through the darkest valley,
I will fear no evil,
　　for you are with me;
your rod and your staff,
　　they comfort me.

You prepare a table before me
　　in the presence of my enemies.
You anoint my head with oil;
　　my cup overflows.
Surely your goodness and love will follow me
　　all the days of my life,
and I will dwell in the house of the LORD
　　forever.

—PSALM 23:1–6

This psalm has been loved because of the comfort it brings to people during times of suffering or loss. It has been quoted at an untold number of funerals.

But like so many other books of the Bible, there are some familiar themes contained there. It's interesting to note that the heroes of the Bible, the leaders and conquerors, are shown to struggle with the same sin problem that we saw at the beginning of the story. The psalms often deal with this sin problem as well. Another well-known chapter is Psalm 51, in which David expresses his grief over his sin.

Have mercy on me, O God,
    according to your unfailing love;
according to your great compassion
    blot out my transgressions.
Wash away all my iniquity
    and cleanse me from my sin.

For I know my transgressions,
    and my sin is always before me.
Against you, you only, have I sinned
    and done what is evil in your sight;
so you are right in your verdict
    and justified when you judge.
Surely I was sinful at birth,
    sinful from the time my mother conceived me.
Yet you desired faithfulness even in the womb;
    you taught me wisdom in that secret place.

Cleanse me with hyssop, and I will be clean;
    wash me, and I will be whiter than snow.
Let me hear joy and gladness;
    let the bones you have crushed rejoice.
Hide your face from my sins
    and blot out all my iniquity.

Create in me a pure heart, O God,
    and renew a steadfast spirit within me.
Do not cast me from your presence
    or take your Holy Spirit from me.

Restore to me the joy of your salvation
and grant me a willing spirit, to sustain me.

Then I will teach transgressors your ways,
so that sinners will turn back to you.
Deliver me from the guilt of bloodshed, O God,
you who are God my Savior,
and my tongue will sing of your righteousness.
Open my lips, Lord,
and my mouth will declare your praise.
You do not delight in sacrifice, or I would bring it;
you do not take pleasure in burnt offerings.
My sacrifice, O God, is a broken spirit;
a broken and contrite heart
you, God, will not despise.

May it please you to prosper Zion,
to build up the walls of Jerusalem.
Then you will delight in the sacrifices of the
righteous,
in burnt offerings offered whole;
then bulls will be offered on your altar.

—PSALM 51:1–19

Notably, Psalm 51 ends with the idea of sacrifice and the need for restoration.

The book of Psalms has 150 chapters. It includes the shortest and the longest chapters in the Bible. There is a variety of topics written about in Psalms. The psalms are written from different perspectives. Some come from deep sorrow, while others are written in times of joy. Some are cries to God for help, and some praise him for his mighty works.

The shortest chapter is Psalm 117. It is a psalm of praise and points out the love of God, which we discussed in chapter 4.

> Praise the LORD, all you nations;
>> extol him, all you peoples.
> For great is his love toward us,
>> and the faithfulness of the LORD endures
>>> forever.
>
> Praise the LORD.
>
> —PSALM 117:1–2

You will find in the psalms reference to the promise God made Abraham, Isaac, and Jacob. Also, the history of the nation of Israel is written about.

In Psalm 105 the writer gives a summary of this history, from Abraham to the Israelites entering the promised land. It starts with praising God: "Give praise to the LORD, proclaim his name; / make known among the nations what he has done" (v. 1). Then, in verses 5–8, the writer recalls the promise God made to Abraham and his descendants:

Remember the wonders he has done,
>his miracles, and the judgments he pronounced,
you his servants, the descendants of Abraham,
>his chosen ones, the children of Jacob.
He is the LORD our God;
>his judgments are in all the earth.

He remembers his covenant forever,
>the promise he made, for a thousand
>>generations.

The psalm goes on to discuss Joseph being sold as a slave, leading to his family, including his father, moving to Egypt.

[The LORD] called down famine on the land
>and destroyed all their supplies of food;
and he sent a man before them—
>Joseph, sold as a slave.
They bruised his feet with shackles,
>his neck was put in irons,
till what he foretold came to pass,
>till the word of the LORD proved him true.

—VERSES 16–19

Then it moves to Moses and the wonders God performed to bring the children of Israel out of Egypt: "[The

LORD] sent Moses his servant, / and Aaron, whom he had chosen. / They performed his signs among them, / his wonders in the land of Ham" (vv. 26–27).

In the end, the writer returns to the promise made to Abraham, before ending the chapter with, "Praise the LORD" (v. 45). Much more could be said, and there have been many books written just on the book of Psalms, but let's move on to another favorite book that comes from this section of the Bible.

THE WISDOM LITERATURE

Let's return to *Bible Gateway*'s most popular books of the Bible. While Psalms came in at number one, the fifth most popular book was Proverbs.

We find a large portion of the book of Proverbs attributed to King Solomon. The book of 2 Chronicles records an encounter Solomon had with God, shortly after David's time as king ended. God told Solomon to ask him for whatever he wanted. Solomon responded by saying, "You have shown great kindness to David my father and have made me king in his place. Now, LORD God, let your promise to my father David be confirmed, for you have made me king over a people who are as numerous as the dust of the earth. Give me wisdom and knowledge, that I may lead this people, for who is able to govern this great people of yours?" (2 Chron. 1:8–10).

Solomon's response pleased God.

"Since this is your heart's desire," said God, "and you have not asked for wealth, possessions or honor, nor for the death of your enemies, and since you have not asked for a long life but for wisdom and knowledge to govern my people over whom I have made you king, therefore wisdom and knowledge will be given you. And I will also give you wealth, possessions and honor, such as no king who was before you ever had and none after you will have" (vv. 11–12).

Solomon was renowned for his vast wealth, but more so for his great wisdom. First Kings 4:31 says this of Solomon: "He was wiser than anyone else, including Ethan the Ezrahite—wiser than Heman, Kalkol and Darda, the sons of Mahol. And his fame spread to all the surrounding nations."

THE "FIT" OF WISDOM LITERATURE

The book of Proverbs offers readers pithy practical advice through the use of poetic couplets. One central theme dominates even from the outset of the book, where Solomon says in Proverbs 1:2–3,

> for gaining wisdom and instruction;
> for understanding words of insight;
> for receiving instruction in prudent behavior,
> doing what is right and just and fair.

Proverbs is essentially a book of instructions on how to live wisely in a world struggling with sin. The book, then, is advice on how to live and act wisely in matters such as raising children, handling money, and working diligently.

THE BOOK OF JOB

The book of Job begins by telling us of Job, a wealthy and prosperous man, a man of status and righteousness. Yet Job loses everything he owns, including all of his children, in a short period. After he hears from two of his servants that his children have been tragically killed, and his herds of livestock stolen, Job mourns.

The Bible says, "Job got up and tore his robe and shaved his head. Then he fell to the ground in worship and said: 'Naked I came from my mother's womb, and naked I will depart. The LORD gave and the LORD has taken away; may the name of the LORD be praised" (Job 1:20–21). Job's wife even tells him to curse God and die because of his awful state of loss and suffering.

Then three of Job's friends show up and offer advice to their friend (Job 4–27). It's not very good advice. They tell Job that because God lets bad things happen only to bad people, Job must be a bad person. But we know from the opening of the book that God considers Job to be a good and righteous man. It is only after a character called Satan suggests God remove the hedge of protection around Job that this calamity comes to him (Job 1).

Rather than encourage their friend, Job's friends blame Job for his state of affairs. But Job does not abandon God or blame God, like his three friends suggest. No. Job is trying to learn from God through the situation. And his friends aren't helping. If anything, they're confusing him.

Then we read a dialogue, spanning six chapters, between Job and a younger man named Elihu.

Elihu waits until Job's three friends speak their piece, because it's customary and respectful for the younger man to wait for his elders to finish before he intervenes. Finally, Elihu gets his turn. And he's angry—angry that Job's friends found no real wisdom to give Job in light of his calamity. But Elihu does not stop there. He confronts Job for how he's handled his awful situation.

But Elihu, in the end, does not offer Job better advice than did the other three friends. Finally, after Elihu finishes his dialogue with Job, God speaks.

God does not condemn Job for lamenting or even cursing his own birth. God does not reprimand Job for his hard questions about the situation or for Job's indignation that sometimes good people suffer while evil people prosper.

Instead God walks Job through some of the most beautifully intense and almost cinematic dialogue in the Bible as he shows Job that life, like God himself, is complicated and hard to understand, and sometimes the answers don't come quickly; sometimes answers never come at all (Job 38–42).

_____

Psalms. Proverbs. Job. Three of the poetry and wisdom books—these today continue to be some of the most loved and most read books of the Bible. They give practical advice for living, yet at the same time return to the themes of dealing with sin and the need for rescue.

TEN

JESUS, THE UNLIKELY KING

As we have seen, the Bible's story, like any story, has a beginning.

In the beginning God created all things, and he called his creation good. But because of the choices Adam and Eve made, the relationship with God was broken, and the result was a world of chaos. God then called a man, Abraham, to build a nation and follow his instructions. We've come to know this nation as Israel.

Rescuing this nation out of Egypt is a story that the nation was to memorialize for future generations so that they would never forget how God delivered them from slavery. It became the annual remembrance called Passover. That was the centerpiece of their exodus from Egypt and began their journey to the land God had promised to them. This Passover story, like Mephibosheth's story, reflects the greater story of the Bible, in which the creator God wants to rescue humanity from that which separates them.

But once in the promised land, the Israelites fight the inhabitants of the land, they fight among themselves, and they fight their God.

How will God rescue humanity?

WHAT HAPPENED BETWEEN THE TESTAMENTS?

Before we unfold more of God's rescue story, it's important to know where we are along the biblical narrative.

On our historical timeline, about four hundred years separate the Old and New Testaments. As we ended the previous chapter, the Northern Kingdom, Israel, was annihilated by Assyria (722 BC), which dispersed many of the remaining Jews from the Northern Kingdom throughout the Middle East. This came to be known as the diaspora—the dispersion.

The Southern Kingdom, Judah, was conquered by the Babylonian Empire, the city of Jerusalem was burned, and the Israelites were forced to live in exile in Babylon. The Israelites were a conquered people, forced to live in a foreign land. During this time of exile, we see prophets such as Daniel and Ezekiel rise to encourage, correct, and challenge the Israelites.

But the Babylon reign was not indefinite; the Persians defeated the Babylonians and allowed a remnant of Israelites from the Southern Kingdom, who were living in exile, to return to their homeland. The prophetic books of Ezra and Nehemiah tell of this return.

Four hundred years later, Rome is now in the picture.

Caesar Augustus is the reigning Roman emperor when Jesus is born. Augustus was known for transforming Rome from a city of clay to a city of marble. A man of great ambition but also politically wise, Caesar Augustus initiated great building projects, and it was his idea to enroll the known world in a census so that all would be taxed. His census and tax decree began the chain of events that forced Jesus' parents, Mary and Joseph, to leave their home in Nazareth and travel to Bethlehem because everyone had to return to the place of their family origin for the census. Bethlehem, known as the City of David, would be the birthplace of Jesus. It was during the reign of Caesar Augustus that the Roman Empire enjoyed a time of great peace known as the *Pax Romana*, or "Roman peace."

The New Testament writer Paul comments on this time when Jesus enters the story of the Bible: "When the fullness of time had come, God sent forth his Son, born of woman, born under the law, to redeem those who were under the law, so that we might receive adoption as sons" (Gal. 4:4–5 ESV).

And so the stage is set for the rescue plan to continue, following the time of the prophets and the kings. The Israelites live as a decentralized people, in Israel and throughout the Middle East and beyond. Caesar Augustus has extended the Roman Empire throughout the known world and brought economic prosperity and peace to the land. The great Roman road system has made travel safer and easier. The Israelites, however, still wait for what the prophets call a messiah—a ruler who will renew their kingdom and lead them out from under the oppression of Rome. With this context in view, let's look at part two of the English Bible—what Christians call the New Testament—and the story of the rescue.

THE NEW TESTAMENT

The New Testament begins with the gospel according to Matthew. Matthew, Mark, Luke, and John write basically the same story but from each author's perspective, detailing the events in the life of Jesus. Matthew is a Jew writing to a Jewish audience and makes connections to the Old Testament, with an eye toward showing Jesus as the promised Messiah, the king of the Jews.

THE GENEALOGY OF
JESUS CHRIST

This is the genealogy of Jesus Christ, with which Matthew begins. Genealogies were used to show family heritage and establish someone's reputation.

Note how Matthew connects the Old Testament—all the way back to Abraham, through the house of David, up to and through the time of exile—to Joseph's family. Keep in mind that Caesar Augustus has just decreed that a census be taken, so Joseph and Mary have to travel back to Joseph's hometown of Bethlehem, the City of David.

This is the genealogy of Jesus the Messiah the son of David, the son of Abraham:

Abraham was the father of Isaac,
Isaac the father of Jacob,
Jacob the father of Judah and his brothers,
Judah the father of Perez and Zerah, whose mother was Tamar,
Perez the father of Hezron,
Hezron the father of Ram,
Ram the father of Amminadab,
Amminadab the father of Nahshon,
Nahshon the father of Salmon,
Salmon the father of Boaz, whose mother was Rahab,

Boaz the father of Obed, whose mother
   was Ruth,
Obed the father of Jesse,
and Jesse the father of King David.

David was the father of Solomon, whose mother
   had been Uriah's wife,
Solomon the father of Rehoboam,
Rehoboam the father of Abijah,
Abijah the father of Asa,
Asa the father of Jehoshaphat,
Jehoshaphat the father of Jehoram,
Jehoram the father of Uzziah,
Uzziah the father of Jotham,
Jotham the father of Ahaz,
Ahaz the father of Hezekiah,
Hezekiah the father of Manasseh,
Manasseh the father of Amon,
Amon the father of Josiah,
and Josiah the father of Jeconiah and his
   brothers at the time of the exile to
   Babylon.

After the exile to Babylon:
Jeconiah was the father of Shealtiel,
Shealtiel the father of Zerubbabel,
Zerubbabel the father of Abihud,
Abihud the father of Eliakim,

Eliakim the father of Azor,
Azor the father of Zadok,
Zadok the father of Akim,
Akim the father of Elihud,
Elihud the father of Eleazar,
Eleazar the father of Matthan,
Matthan the father of Jacob,
and Jacob the father of Joseph, the husband
   of Mary, and Mary was the mother of
   Jesus who is called the Messiah.

Thus there were fourteen generations in all from Abraham to David, fourteen from David to the exile to Babylon, and fourteen from the exile to the Messiah.
—MATTHEW 1:1–17

Matthew refers to Joseph as a son of David, which was a meaningful phrase to his Jewish audience, for they knew and lived with anticipation that the Messiah would come from the line of David: "An angel of the Lord appeared to him in a dream and said, 'Joseph son of David, do not be afraid to take Mary home as your wife, because what is conceived in her is from the Holy Spirit'" (Matt. 1:20).

Later, Matthew writes of the people considering who this Jesus might be: "All the people were astonished and said, 'Could this be the Son of David?'" (Matt. 12:23).

Elsewhere in the Gospels, John also emphasizes the connection between David and Jesus: "Does not Scripture say that the Messiah will come from David's descendants and from Bethlehem, the town where David lived?" (John 7:42).

The apostle Paul also gets into the action, in his letter to the Romans: "Paul, a servant of Christ Jesus, called to be an apostle and set apart for the gospel of God—the gospel he promised beforehand through his prophets in the Holy Scriptures regarding his Son, who as to his earthly life was a descendant of David, and who through the Spirit of holiness was appointed the Son of God in power by his resurrection from the dead: Jesus Christ our Lord" (Rom. 1:1–4). While Matthew's genealogy might feel cumbersome to read, it shows that Jesus fulfills the prediction that the Messiah would come from David.

One emphasis of the gospel of Mark is to make the story of Jesus relatable to Gentiles (non-Jews). It is short, fast-paced, and easy to understand.[10] In the book of Luke, the stated purpose is to give readers an orderly and accurate picture of Jesus' life. The book of John, the last of the gospel accounts, takes a more theological approach to the life of Jesus, emphasizing Jesus as the divine Son of God.[11]

As I've noted, these first four books are referred to as the Gospels—the word gospel meaning "good news," or "joyous tidings"—because of their focus on the ministry of Jesus, which includes his death and resurrection.

After the Gospels, the next book, called Acts, tells of the deeds of the followers of Jesus. It primarily focuses on two of Jesus' followers: Peter, who, during the time of Jesus' trial, denied he knew him; and Saul, who was also known as Paul, and who had persecuted followers of Jesus. It was while Saul was on his way to Damascus to arrest followers of Jesus that he was blinded by God and called to follow "the Way" (Christianity; see Acts 9:1–2) of those he was persecuting. We will discuss this book in the next chapter.

Following Acts, we find the books of the Bible referred to as letters. The letters were written to various audiences, addressing issues related to daily living and what was expected of the "church" (all followers of Jesus; see Matt. 16:17–18) when they gathered for worship. The letters also addressed questions that became relevant for those who believed that Jesus was the Messiah, things like how his death and resurrection had ended the sacrificial system because he paid the penalty once and for all for the sins of humanity.

The last book of the New Testament is the book of Revelation. It is set apart and unique. It starts by saying it is the revelation of Jesus Christ that God gave to John by way of an angel. Its stated purpose is "to show to his servants the things that must soon take place" (Rev. 1:1 ESV).

Now that we've looked over the historical timeline and sketched a bit of the New Testament, let's get back to the story.

JESUS OF NAZARETH

The New Testament is about Jesus, and the final week of his life is what attracts much of the attention. Roughly one-third of the four gospels deals with this week. So though Jesus' life is recorded to have lasted thirty-three years, it is this one week on which all four writers focus. The primary events are Jesus' trial before Pontius Pilate, his death by way of crucifixion on a Roman cross, his burial in the tomb of a wealthy Jew, and his resurrection on the third day.

The book of Matthew, the gospel account that opens the New Testament, begins by tracing the family tree of Jesus. Earlier, we saw that the prophecies given throughout the Old Testament show that there is a continuation of the story that was started at the beginning of the Bible, and that the story is continued through a family line.

We begin with the very first line of the first book of the New Testament. Matthew 1:1 says, "The book of the genealogy of Jesus Christ, the son of David, the son of Abraham" (ESV). Genealogy serves to connect the past to the present. Similarly, the New Testament ties itself to the Old Testament through its main character, Jesus. After this first line, Matthew gives the genealogy of Jesus, starting with Abraham and going through David to Joseph, the husband of Mary, the mother of Jesus. (See sidebar "The Genealogy of Jesus Christ.")

In the book of Matthew, there are many instances

of Jesus being called the son of David. In one case, he is walking by two blind men, and they call out, "Lord, Son of David" (Matt. 20:30). At another time, there is a Canaanite woman who has a demon-oppressed daughter, crying out, "O Lord, Son of David" (Matt. 15:22 ESV). Even the angel who appears to Joseph in a dream and tells him to take Mary as his wife refers to Jesus as the son of David. The connection is hard to miss, and the genealogy of Jesus is just the beginning of the connection.

The Bible doesn't say too much about Jesus' life from his birth until his public teaching began when he was about thirty years old. There's one verse in Luke's gospel account that sheds a little light: "Jesus grew in wisdom and stature, and in favor with God and man" (Luke 2:52). Otherwise, the emphasis is on a few years of the life of Jesus.

REMEMBER PROPHECY?

In the New Testament, the writers regularly point back to prophecies in the Old Testament, claiming that they are being fulfilled. These prophecies—and specifically, the prophecies concerning Jesus—connect the Old and New Testaments. The Israelites were looking for the one who was to come, a messiah, or as Moses put it, a prophet like him, or as David was told, a leader who would follow him and whose throne would be established forever.

At the time of Jesus' birth, wise men from the east

were seeking the "king of the Jews" (Matt. 2:2) because they saw his star and wanted to worship him. When they came to Jerusalem, they asked King Herod where he might be.

Herod was a ruthless and intelligent king who ruled for Caesar. He was in charge of keeping this province in peaceful order. But he was no one to trifle with. Since he had been made the king of Judea, he wanted to know where the supposed king of the Jews was to be born, but not so he could pay his respects; he was bent on keeping his throne. He checked with the chief priests and scribes, those who would know the Jewish Scriptures, and they told him the answer.

They told him this king would be born in Bethlehem of Judea, because that is where the prophets of previous times said he would be born. The account in Matthew then quotes a portion of the Old Testament book written by the prophet Micah.

> You, O Bethlehem Ephrathah,
>   who are too little to be among the clans of
>   Judah,
> from you shall come forth for me
>   one who is to be ruler in Israel,
>   whose coming forth is from of old,
>   from ancient days.
>
> —MICAH 5:2 ESV

According to the biblical timeline, Micah prophesied around seven hundred years before the birth of Jesus.

Herod then told the wise men where Jesus could be found and asked them to let him know when they located the child, because he wanted to worship the child as well. This, of course, was a lie. The wise men, however, were warned in a dream not to return to Herod as he had asked, so after they visited and worshiped Jesus, they returned home via another route (Matt. 2:12).

When Herod realized they had tricked him, he became angry. He was a jealous king and fond of his power and position, and he'd do whatever he could to keep it. So in an effort to kill Jesus, whom the wise men had come to worship by way of giving him gifts, he ordered that all the male children two years old and under in the region of Bethlehem be killed.

Consider Herod's act and how it affected Mary and Joseph.

The Bible says that an angel warned Joseph of the coming massacre and told him to flee with Mary and Jesus: "When [the wise men] had gone, an angel of the Lord appeared to Joseph in a dream. 'Get up,' he said, 'take the child and his mother and escape to Egypt. Stay there until I tell you, for Herod is going to search for the child to kill him'" (Matt. 2:13).

This unthinkable and brutal action taken by Herod, Matthew says, was fulfilling another prophecy, one given in the book of Jeremiah, which was written more than six hundred years before Jesus' birth.

> Thus says the LORD:
> "A voice is heard in Ramah,
>   lamentation and bitter weeping.
> Rachel is weeping for her children;
>   she refuses to be comforted for her children,
>   because they are no more."
> —JEREMIAH 31:15 ESV

Though Jesus was born in a time of great peace and economic prosperity under Roman rule, the nation of Israel was desperate for a new king—their own king who would reestablish Jewish sovereignty in their own land. The local ruler, Herod, was desperate to remain as such. It was an unsafe time for Jesus individually, and a scary time for Mary and Joseph. God had given them the task of parenting this child, but it was anything but easy.

The New Testament writers claim that from his birth Jesus is the one prophesied in the Old Testament. He is the king of the Jews.

JOHN THE BAPTIST

Among the first to recognize Jesus as the one who was prophesied about in the Old Testament was John the

Baptist. All four gospel writers write about him. Mary, the mother of Jesus, was related to Elizabeth, the mother of John the Baptist. The book of Mark starts right off saying that John the Baptist himself was prophesied about in the book of Isaiah. Here is how Mark's gospel starts.

The beginning of the good news about Jesus the Messiah, the Son of God, as it is written in Isaiah the prophet:

"I will send my messenger ahead of you,
    who will prepare your way"—
"a voice of one calling in the wilderness,
'Prepare the way for the Lord,
    make straight paths for him.'"

And so John the Baptist appeared in the wilderness, preaching a baptism of repentance for the forgiveness of sins. The whole Judean countryside and all the people of Jerusalem went out to him. Confessing their sins, they were baptized by him in the Jordan River. John wore clothing made of camel's hair, with a leather belt around his waist, and he ate locusts and wild honey. And this was his message: "After me comes the one more powerful than I, the straps of whose sandals I am not worthy to stoop down and untie. I baptize you with water, but he will baptize you with the Holy Spirit."

—MARK 1:1–8

When John the Baptist arrived on the scene, some people asked if *he* was the Christ—the Messiah—prophesied by Isaiah. John the Baptist, however, made it clear that though he himself had been prophesied about, he was not the Christ. The Christ was coming and indeed had come, and John the Baptist knew this and was looking for him with anticipation. He noted how Jesus was the prophesied king they all were searching for and yet he was humble in stature, wearing sandals like any common man or woman. A different kind of king was coming.

Matthew quotes from this same passage in Isaiah that foretells of John the Baptist. John's account records John the Baptist himself using the same passage when asked who he was. Also in the book of John, John the Baptist states clearly that he recognizes Jesus as the Christ.

> The next day John saw Jesus coming toward him and said, "Look, the Lamb of God, who takes away the sin of the world! This is the one I meant when I said, 'A man who comes after me has surpassed me because he was before me.' I myself did not know him, but the reason I came baptizing with water was that he might be revealed to Israel."
>
> Then John gave this testimony: "I saw the Spirit come down from heaven as a dove and remain on him. And I myself did not know him, but the one who sent me to baptize with water told me, 'The man on whom

you see the Spirit come down and remain is the one
who will baptize with the Holy Spirit.' I have seen and
I testify that this is God's Chosen One."

—JOHN 1:29–34

What did John the Baptist mean when he said,
"Behold, the Lamb of God, who takes away the sin of the
world!" (John 1:29 ESV)? Was he saying that Jesus was
the answer to the sin problem that started in the garden
of Eden? How was Jesus a lamb of God? Was John saying
Jesus was a lamb like the Passover lamb?

John the Baptist is not the only one who saw Jesus
in a special light. There are many instances in which the
New Testament writers look back into the Old Testament,
pointing out the continuation of the one story. Let's look
at some.

ISAIAH 53

One particular portion of the Old Testament is referred
to by several writers of the New Testament: Isaiah 53.
Isaiah, who comes before Jeremiah and Ezekiel in our
biblical timeline (see sidebar), prophesied about a servant
and a king. The New Testament writers claim that Jesus
is the fulfillment of Isaiah's prophecy, which had, according to the biblical timeline, occurred approximately seven
hundred years beforehand.

TIMELINE OF THE MAJOR PROPHETS OF THE OLD TESTAMENT

Isaiah: 701–681 BC
Jeremiah: 626–582 BC
Ezekiel: 593–571 BC
Daniel: 605–535 BC

Let's take a look at what Isaiah says in chapter 53 and then the New Testament connections to it.

> Who has believed what he has heard from us?
>   And to whom has the arm of the LORD been
>   revealed?
> For he grew up before him like a young plant,
>   and like a root out of dry ground;
> he had no form or majesty that we should look
>   at him,
>   and no beauty that we should desire him.
> He was despised and rejected by men,
>   a man of sorrows and acquainted with grief;
> and as one from whom men hide their faces
>   he was despised, and we esteemed him not.
>
> Surely he has borne our griefs
>   and carried our sorrows;

yet we esteemed him stricken,
    smitten by God, and afflicted.
But he was pierced for our transgressions;
    he was crushed for our iniquities;
upon him was the chastisement that brought us
      peace,
    and with his wounds we are healed.
All we like sheep have gone astray;
    we have turned—every one—to his own way;
and the Lord has laid on him
    the iniquity of us all.

He was oppressed, and he was afflicted,
    yet he opened not his mouth;
like a lamb that is led to the slaughter,
    and like a sheep that before its shearers is silent,
    so he opened not his mouth.
By oppression and judgment he was taken away;
    and as for his generation, who considered
that he was cut off out of the land of the living,
    stricken for the transgression of my people?
And they made his grave with the wicked
    and with a rich man in his death,
although he had done no violence,
    and there was no deceit in his mouth.

Yet it was the will of the Lord to crush him;
    he has put him to grief;

when his soul makes an offering for guilt,
> he shall see his offspring; he shall prolong
> > his days;
the will of the LORD shall prosper in his hand.
Out of the anguish of his soul he shall see and be
> satisfied;
by his knowledge shall the righteous one, my
> servant,
> > make many to be accounted righteous,
> > and he shall bear their iniquities.
Therefore I will divide him a portion with the many,
> and he shall divide the spoil with the strong,
because he poured out his soul to death
> and was numbered with the transgressors;
yet he bore the sin of many,
> and makes intercession for the transgressors.
> > > —ISAIAH 53:1–12 ESV

In six different passages of the New Testament, the writers reference that Jesus was who Isaiah 53 was prophesying about. Both the book of John and the book of Romans point to Isaiah 53:1. As John recounts the latter part of Jesus' life, he tells some of what Jesus taught and then writes the following, quoting Isaiah 53:1.

"Believe in the light while you have the light, so that you may become children of light." When he had finished speaking, Jesus left and hid himself from [the crowd].

Even after Jesus had performed so many signs in their presence, they still would not believe in him. This was to fulfill the word of Isaiah the prophet:

"Lord, who has believed our message
and to whom has the arm of the Lord been
revealed?"

—JOHN 12:36–38

Paul, writing in the book of Romans, also speaks of those who do not believe in Jesus and quotes the same verse in Isaiah. "Not all the Israelites accepted the good news. For Isaiah says, 'Lord, who has believed our message?'" (Rom. 10:16).

Matthew refers to Isaiah 53:4 as he tells how Jesus healed many. "This was to fulfill what was spoken through the prophet Isaiah: 'He took up our infirmities and bore our diseases'" (Matt. 8:17).

Though Peter does not specifically mention Isaiah, like the other writers we have looked at, he refers to verses 4, 5, 6, 7, and 9 of the fifty-third chapter of Isaiah as he is writing of Jesus. "'He committed no sin, and no deceit was found in his mouth' [v. 9]. When they hurled their insults at him, he did not retaliate [v. 7]; when he suffered, he made no threats. Instead, he entrusted himself to him who judges justly. 'He himself bore our sins' in his body on the cross [v. 4], so that we might die to sins and live for righteousness; 'by his wounds you have been healed' [v. 5]. For 'you were like sheep going astray' [v. 6], but now you have returned to the Shepherd and Overseer of your souls" (1 Peter 2:22–25).

It is during the last meal he will eat with his disciples before his crucifixion—the Passover meal we discussed, known as the Last Supper—that Jesus himself refers to Isaiah 53, when he indicates he will be "numbered with the transgressors." This is a reference to the twelfth verse of Isaiah 53, which prophesies his death among criminals. Jesus says, "It is written: 'And he was numbered with the transgressors'; and I tell you that this must be fulfilled in me. Yes, what is written about me is reaching its fulfillment" (Luke 22:37).

There are other verses we could look at that are not as direct in referring to Isaiah's prophecy, but I think this is sufficient to make the point. We looked at five writers who pointed to Isaiah 53, one who was quoting Jesus himself claiming he is the one that Isaiah was prophesying about. The sixth reference we will look at in the next chapter.

MORE CONNECTIONS

While there are more specific references we could look at, there are also general comments that indicate the New Testament is a continuation of the story started in the Old Testament. Paul starts the book of Romans by connecting both prophecy about Jesus and David's genealogy to the New Testament. "Paul, a servant of Christ Jesus, called to be an apostle and set apart for the gospel of God— the gospel he promised beforehand through his prophets in the Holy Scriptures regarding his Son, who as to his earthly life was a descendant of David, and who through the Spirit of holiness was appointed the Son of God in power by his resurrection from the dead: Jesus Christ our Lord" (Rom. 1:1–4).

In the book of John, we have an interesting comment by Philip, who says of Jesus, "We have found him of whom Moses in the Law and also the prophets wrote, Jesus of Nazareth, the son of Joseph" (John 1:45 ESV). This claim is early in the life of Jesus, and already Philip is connecting Jesus to the writings of Moses and the prophets! This happens soon after John the Baptist recognizes who Jesus is.

And look at what Jesus says about himself. John quotes Jesus as saying, "If you believed Moses, you would believe me; for he wrote of me" (John 5:46 ESV).

The book of Luke records an event, on the day of Jesus' resurrection, in which he comes upon two men walking on the road to Emmaus. Jesus asks what they are talking about. They are despondent and report of Jesus' death. They also report of Jesus' tomb being found empty. Luke says this was Jesus' response: "He said to them, 'How foolish you are, and how slow to believe all that the prophets have spoken! Did not the Messiah have to suffer these things and then enter his glory?' And beginning with Moses and all the Prophets, he explained to them what was said in all the Scriptures concerning himself" (Luke 24:25–27).

Later in the same chapter of Luke, when Jesus is with his disciples, he repeats the claim. "He said to them, 'This is what I told you while I was still with you: Everything must be fulfilled that is written about me in the Law of Moses, the Prophets and the Psalms'" (Luke 24:44).

So from specific references to Isaiah in the Old Testament to general comments, we find Jesus and others pointing out that Jesus is the one the prophets were talking about. There are also verses that are vague but, some would say, point to Jesus. Do you remember the very first prophecy we discussed, in the book of Genesis, where it says this:

> "I will put enmity
>   between you and the woman,
>   and between your offspring and hers;
> he will crush your head,
>   and you will strike his heel."
>
> —GENESIS 3:15

Some see this as pointing to Jesus and his resurrection. The serpent struck Jesus' heel by orchestrating his death on the cross, yet Jesus crushed the serpent's head by rising from the dead.

To list all the potential—specific and implied—references to Jesus in the Old Testament is not the intent of this book. I just want to address enough of these connections to make a simple point: the New Testament's story is that Jesus is the fulfillment of what was prophesied in the Old Testament.

THE PASSOVER LAMB

So how does Jesus fit into the story of the Bible?

That takes us back to the Passover. We discussed that the Passover is the essence of the Bible's story. The Passover, like the story of Mephibosheth, points to *the* story of the Bible—the story of how Jesus is the Passover lamb, how he is the one whose life was sacrificed so that others might live.

When John the Baptist sees Jesus coming, he says, "Behold, the Lamb of God, who takes away the sin of the world!" (John 1:29 ESV). That is what the story of the Bible is all about: the story of humanity's sin problem that started in the garden of Eden, and how it was resolved by Jesus becoming the Passover lamb, paying the price for man's sin.

This sacrifice for man's sin is called a gift, meaning it can be accepted or not. One analogy is that Jesus stands at the door and knocks (Rev. 3:20), meaning he doesn't force his way in. He lets his creation choose whether to open the door, just as God gave Adam and Eve the choice in the garden. If the sacrificial lamb's blood is on the doorposts in Egypt, or if the blood that Jesus shed is accepted, man can be saved from his sin.

That, in essence, is the story of the Bible. It points to Jesus resolving the sin problem and making a way to restore the relationship man had with God in the garden. Through Jesus, a descendant of Abraham, all the nations of the earth will be blessed. He is the prophet to come of whom Moses prophesied, and he is the son of David whose kingdom will last forever.

Is that really what the Bible says, or am I reading more into the story than what is meant? Let's see what the followers of Jesus say in the next chapter.

ELEVEN

THE SPREAD OF
THE GOOD NEWS

The New Testament says that unlike the Passover lamb in the Old Testament, Jesus was the perfect lamb. His death created a way for death to be overcome by those who believe in him. Likewise, the blood of Jesus made a way to live reunited with God.

It says that three days after Jesus was placed in the tomb, he rose again. On the third day after Jesus was put to death on a Roman cross, one of his followers, a woman named Mary Magdalene, walked to the tomb in the early morning darkness, and as she approached, she noticed that the massive stone placed over the entrance had been rolled away. She ran back to town to tell the other disciples. "They have taken the Lord out of the tomb," she said, "and we don't know where they have put him!" (John 20:2).

Peter and John, two of Jesus' closest disciples, ran to the tomb with Mary and discovered it was just as Mary had reported. The tomb was empty. The Bible says Peter stepped into the tomb and inspected the linens that had wrapped Jesus' body. When John looked into the tomb and walked inside, we're told, he "saw and believed" (v. 8).

Peter and John ran back to tell the other followers of Jesus. Mary stayed outside the tomb and wept. As she looked into the tomb with tears in her eyes, she saw two angels sitting there.

"Woman, why are you crying?" the angels asked her (v. 13).

"They have taken my Lord away," she said to them, "and I don't know where they have put him" (v. 13).

Then Mary turned from the tomb and saw Jesus standing there, but she did not realize that it was him.

"Woman, why are you crying?" said Jesus to Mary. "Who is it you are looking for?" (v. 15).

But Mary thought he was the gardener and said, "Sir, if you have carried him away, tell me where you have put him, and I will get him" (v. 15).

Then Jesus called her by name.

"Mary," he said (v. 16).

At once Mary recognized that it was Jesus.

"Teacher!"

Jesus said, "Do not hold on to me, for I have not yet ascended to the Father. Go instead to my brothers and tell them, 'I am ascending to my Father and your Father, to my God and your God'" (v. 17).

Mary left the tomb and went to the disciples and said, "I have seen the Lord!" (v. 18).

Later, the apostle Paul would write a letter to the Corinthian church and explain to them that over the course of the forty days after Jesus appeared to Mary and his disciples, Jesus would show himself to more than five hundred people (1 Cor. 15:6). John says that Jesus "performed many other signs in the presence of his disciples, which are not recorded in this book. But these are written that you may believe that Jesus is the Messiah, the Son of God, and that by believing you may have life in his name" (John 20:30–31).

Before Jesus left the disciples and was taken up into heaven, he assured them that he would not leave them alone; the Comforter, or Holy Spirit, would come. And his presence would be the same as having Jesus himself with them, only better. And the Holy Spirit would be available to all who believe. (See John 14:15–31.)

He also said to them, "All authority in heaven and on earth has been given to me" (Matt. 28:18).

After he made this declaration to the disciples, he told

them to go into their world and preach the gospel. And then he ascended into heaven, and "a cloud hid him from their sight" (Acts 1:9). He was gone, back to heaven to be with the Father. The disciples were standing there, staring up into the sky, when two men dressed in white appeared beside them.

"Men of Galilee," they said, "why do you stand here looking into the sky? This same Jesus, who has been taken from you into heaven, will come back in the same way you have seen him go into heaven" (Acts 1:10–12).

So now what? What did preaching the good news look like? And now that Jesus was gone, how would his followers react? Would they pack up and head home? Or would they do what he told them to do?

The book of Acts records how the message of Jesus' death and resurrection spread and how the church grew because the disciples and new converts began preaching the things Jesus taught during his life on earth.

Let's look at three sermons and a story that show us what Jesus' followers were saying about the events they had just witnessed.

PETER SPEAKS IN SOLOMON'S PORTICO

Peter and John are walking to the temple to pray. It is three o'clock in the afternoon. They encounter a crippled man sitting by the temple gate who asks the two disciples for money. Peter says, "I don't have money to give you, but I can give something else." Peter takes the man by the hand and tells him, "By the power of Jesus Christ of Nazareth, get up and walk." The man's feet and ankles become strong, and he rises and walks.

He walks with Peter and John into the temple courts, the whole time jumping up and down and praising God. When the people at the temple see this, they come rushing over to see what happened. Peter takes the opportunity, even while the healed man is still clinging to him, to tell the joyous tidings of Jesus of Nazareth.

> "Fellow Israelites, why does this surprise you? Why do you stare at us as if by our own power or godliness we had made this man walk? The God of Abraham, Isaac and Jacob, the God of our fathers, has glorified his servant Jesus. You handed him over to be killed, and you disowned him before Pilate, though he had decided to let him go. You disowned the Holy and Righteous One and asked that a murderer be released to you. You killed the author of life, but God raised him from the dead. We are witnesses of this."
>
> —ACTS 3:12–15

With those words, Peter immediately connects the God of the Old Testament with Jesus, and then he recounts the recent events that took place with Jesus and the crucifixion.

"By faith in the name of Jesus, this man whom you see and know was made strong. It is Jesus' name and the faith that comes through him that has completely healed him, as you can all see.

"Now, fellow Israelites, I know that you acted in ignorance, as did your leaders. But this is how God fulfilled what he had foretold through all the prophets, saying that his Messiah would suffer."

—ACTS 3:16–18

Here he connects the crucifixion of Jesus with the message from the prophets in the Old Testament. He's connecting the dots for his audience.

"Repent, then, and turn to God, so that your sins may be wiped out, that times of refreshing may come from the Lord, and that he may send the Messiah, who has been appointed for you—even Jesus. Heaven must receive him until the time comes for God to restore everything, as he promised long ago through his holy prophets. For Moses said, 'The Lord your God will raise up for you a prophet like me from among your own people; you must listen to everything he tells you. Anyone who does not listen to him will be completely cut off from their people.'

"Indeed, beginning with Samuel, all the prophets who have spoken have foretold these days. And you are heirs of the prophets and of the covenant God made with your fathers. He said to Abraham, 'Through your off-spring all peoples on earth will be blessed.' When God raised up his servant, he sent him first to you to bless you by turning each of you from your wicked ways."

—ACTS 3:19–26

Peter reminds them of the promise God made to Abraham, along with the promise of a prophet like Moses, and then claims that these promises have been fulfilled by and through Jesus. I find it interesting that after the healing of this crippled man, the religious leaders of the day attributed the boldness of Peter and John to their having been with Jesus (Acts 4:13).

STEPHEN'S MESSAGE

The message of Stephen highlights the disobedience and rebellion of the children of Israel. Stephen was one of the first deacons appointed in the church, and he also became the church's first martyr. But before he lost his life because of his faith, he gave a stirring sermon to the Jewish religious leaders.

Some people began arguing with Stephen after they heard him preach the gospel and perform "great wonders and signs among the people" (Acts 6:8). But the people who argued with Stephen found it difficult, because the Holy Spirit filled him with wisdom. As a result, they made up stories about him—kind of like bringing trumped-up charges against someone—saying he was blaspheming Moses and God.

They brought Stephen to the religious leaders and produced false witnesses to testify against him. And as they looked at Stephen, the Bible says, his face was like the face of an angel. And then Stephen preached his famous sermon. He summarized the history of Israel, starting with Abraham, going on to discuss Joseph and Moses, and ending by stating that Jesus was the Righteous One who had been predicted. We'll pick up the discussion at the point where Stephen talked about Moses.

"This is the same Moses they had rejected with the words, 'Who made you ruler and judge?' He was sent to be their ruler and deliverer by God himself, through the angel who appeared to him in the bush. He led them out of Egypt and performed wonders and signs in Egypt, at the Red Sea and for forty years in the wilderness.

"This is the Moses who told the Israelites, 'God will raise up for you a prophet like me from your own people.' He was in the assembly in the wilderness, with the angel who spoke to him on Mount Sinai, and with our ancestors; and he received living words to pass on to us.

"But our ancestors refused to obey him. Instead, they rejected him and in their hearts turned back to Egypt. They told Aaron, 'Make us gods who will go before us. As for this fellow Moses who led us out of Egypt—we don't know what has happened to him!' That was the time they made an idol in the form of a calf. They brought sacrifices to it and reveled in what their own hands had made. But God turned away from them and gave them over to the worship of the sun, moon and stars. This agrees with what is written in the book of the prophets:

"'Did you bring me sacrifices and offerings
    forty years in the wilderness, people of Israel?
You have taken up the tabernacle of Molek
    and the star of your god Rephan,
    the idols you made to worship.
Therefore I will send you into exile' beyond Babylon.

"Our ancestors had the tabernacle of the covenant law with them in the wilderness. It had been made as God directed Moses, according to the pattern he had seen. After receiving the tabernacle, our ancestors under Joshua brought it with them when they took the land from the nations God drove out before them. It remained in the land until the time of David, who enjoyed God's favor and asked that he might provide a dwelling place for the God of Jacob. But it was Solomon who built a house for him.

"However, the Most High does not live in houses made by human hands. As the prophet says:

"'Heaven is my throne,
    and the earth is my footstool.
What kind of house will you build for me?
    says the Lord.
    Or where will my resting place be?
Has not my hand made all these things?'

"You stiff-necked people! Your hearts and ears are still uncircumcised. You are just like your ancestors: You always resist the Holy Spirit! Was there ever a prophet your ancestors did not persecute? They even killed those who predicted the coming of the Righteous One. And now you have betrayed and murdered him— you who have received the law that was given through angels but have not obeyed it."

—ACTS 7:35–53

Stephen's sermon did not do him any favors with the religious leaders. When he finished his sermon, the leaders were furious and screamed at him. But Stephen looked up to heaven and said, "Look, I see heaven open and the Son of Man standing at the right hand of God" (Acts 7:56).

This sent them over the top. They dragged Stephen out of the city and stoned him to death. A young man named Saul watched Stephen's stoning and stood by while he died.

The stoning, however, did not silence the gospel message. The Bible says that it was a catalyst that greatly spread the joyous tidings of Jesus. A mass persecution broke out, and the church—anyone who had accepted the gospel of Jesus—scattered all throughout Judea and Samaria.

PHILIP AND THE ETHIOPIAN EUNUCH

The next story that relates to the spread of the gospel message is about another one of the first deacons of the church. Philip was among the seven chosen as deacons, along with Stephen (Acts 6:5), and when the persecution broke out after Stephen's stoning, Philip was one of the followers of Jesus who left Jerusalem and went to Samaria to preach the gospel message.

Philip preached to crowds or individuals in cities, in towns, and on the road. He also performed signs and wonders (Acts 8:5–12). Here's the story of Philip's encounter with an Ethiopian eunuch.

Now an angel of the Lord said to Philip, "Go south to the road—the desert road—that goes down from Jerusalem to Gaza." So he started out, and on his way he met an Ethiopian eunuch, an important official in charge of all the treasury of the Kandake (which means "queen of the Ethiopians"). This man had gone to Jerusalem to worship, and on his way home was sitting in his chariot reading the Book of Isaiah the prophet. The Spirit told Philip, "Go to that chariot and stay near it."

Then Philip ran up to the chariot and heard the man reading Isaiah the prophet. "Do you understand what you are reading?" Philip asked.

"How can I," he said, "unless someone explains it to me?" So he invited Philip to come up and sit with him.

This is the passage of Scripture the eunuch was reading:

> "He was led like a sheep to the slaughter,
>   and as a lamb before its shearer is silent,
>   so he did not open his mouth.
> In his humiliation he was deprived of justice.
>   Who can speak of his descendants?
>   For his life was taken from the earth."

The eunuch asked Philip, "Tell me, please, who is the prophet talking about, himself or someone else?" Then Philip began with that very passage of Scripture and told him the good news about Jesus.

—ACTS 8:26–35

Notice, here is the sixth New Testament reference to Isaiah 53. We looked at five in the previous chapter. In the same way that Jesus used the Old Testament to reveal himself to the two men on the road to Emmaus, Philip used the text of the Old Testament—specifically, the text from Isaiah that talks about the man who was "led like a lamb to the slaughter" (Isa. 53:7)—to tell the eunuch about Jesus.

As they rode along in the chariot, the eunuch saw some water, and he asked Philip to baptize him. So he was baptized and believed in the message of Jesus. The gospel message spread. By going to Samaria and listening to the Holy Spirit, Philip took the good news to the courts of the Ethiopian queen.

THE MESSAGE OF PAUL

Next we find the message of Paul. What's interesting about Paul is, he was the same man we saw earlier, standing by and watching the religious leaders kill Stephen. Then he was known as Saul. But Jesus appeared to him as he was traveling to Damascus. A blast of light shook Saul and blinded him for a period of time. Then the Spirit of the Lord led a man named Ananias to go and lay his hands on Saul that he might regain his sight. Ananias reluctantly did and Saul became a follower of Jesus.

Paul, the man who initially persecuted the early Christians, is credited with writing a majority of the New Testament books.

One Sabbath day, Paul visited a Jewish synagogue in a town called Antioch. After the religious leaders read from the Law and the Prophets, they invited Paul to speak a word of exhortation to the congregants. Note how Paul connected the Old Testament promises to David with the work of Jesus' death and resurrection.

"Fellow Israelites and you Gentiles who worship God, listen to me! The God of the people of Israel chose our ancestors; he made the people prosper during their stay in Egypt; with mighty power he led them out of that country; for about forty years he endured their conduct in the wilderness; and he overthrew seven nations in Canaan, giving their land to his people as their inheritance. All this took about 450 years.

"After this, God gave them judges until the time of Samuel the prophet. Then the people asked for a king, and he gave them Saul son of Kish, of the tribe of Benjamin, who ruled forty years. After removing Saul, he made David their king. God testified concerning him: 'I have found David son of Jesse, a man after my own heart; he will do everything I want him to do.'

"From this man's descendants God has brought to Israel the Savior Jesus, as he promised. Before the coming of Jesus, John preached repentance and baptism to all the people of Israel. As John was completing his work, he said: 'Who do you suppose I am? I am not the one you are looking for. But there is one coming after me whose sandals I am not worthy to untie.'

"Fellow children of Abraham and you God-fearing

Gentiles, it is to us that this message of salvation has been sent. The people of Jerusalem and their rulers did not recognize Jesus, yet in condemning him they fulfilled the words of the prophets that are read every Sabbath. Though they found no proper ground for a death sentence, they asked Pilate to have him executed. When they had carried out all that was written about him, they took him down from the cross and laid him in a tomb. But God raised him from the dead, and for many days he was seen by those who had traveled with him from Galilee to Jerusalem. They are now his witnesses to our people.

"We tell you the good news: What God promised our ancestors he has fulfilled for us, their children, by raising up Jesus. As it is written in the second Psalm:

"'You are my son;
today I have become your father.'

God raised him from the dead so that he will never be subject to decay. As God has said,

"'I will give you the holy and sure blessings promised to David.'

So it is also stated elsewhere:

"'You will not let your holy one see decay.'

"Now when David had served God's purpose in his own generation, he fell asleep; he was buried with his ancestors and his body decayed. But the one whom God raised from the dead did not see decay.

"Therefore, my friends, I want you to know that through Jesus the forgiveness of sins is proclaimed to you. Through him everyone who believes is set free from every sin, a justification you were not able to obtain under the law of Moses. Take care that what the prophets have said does not happen to you:

"'Look, you scoffers,
    wonder and perish,
for I am going to do something in your days
    that you would never believe,
    even if someone told you.'"

—ACTS 13:16–41

The sin problem that started in the garden of Eden had now found its resolution. The promise to David of a throne that would last forever was fulfilled in Jesus. This was the gospel, or good news, that Jesus' disciples began to share everywhere they went.

From these three messages and the story of the Ethiopian eunuch, we can see that the followers of Jesus were telling people that Jesus was the fulfillment of the promises made to Abraham, Moses, and David and that he fulfilled the prophecy of the prophet Isaiah.

This implied that a new day had come, that Jesus brought a new covenant, which is what the term New Testament means. This new covenant created questions.

What was to be done with the old covenant?

Had anything changed?

Things had changed.

Jesus said, "Do not think that I have come to abolish the Law or the Prophets; I have not come to abolish them but to fulfill them" (Matt. 5:17).

What did that mean for those who wanted to follow the law? Let's look at one example, the Passover. Remember, Passover was to be observed every year as a memorial of God rescuing the Israelites from their enslavement at the hand of the Egyptians.

The New Testament says that Jesus is "the Lamb of God, who takes away the sin of the world" (John 1:29).

The Passover lamb was a foreshadowing of what Jesus was ultimately going to do through his death and resurrection. So Jesus fulfilled the law and nullified the need for an annual sacrifice celebrating the Passover. This also applied to the other sacrifices required by the law in the Old Testament; they were no longer needed.[12]

This new way of life being adopted and spread by the followers of Jesus is what the letters following the book of Acts are trying to address.

As this fledgling effort continues, the Bible records, other churches in addition to the church in Jerusalem are established in surrounding cities and countries. Paul assembles his own team and takes the gospel to surrounding nations. Those travels take him to places like Greece, Turkey, and Italy. Paul writes letters of instructions to the churches established there. Those letters, or epistles, come to represent different books of the Bible, such as Romans, Galatians, Ephesians, Colossians, and Philippians.

And finally, the Bible concludes with the culminating book called Revelation. This book can be summed up as a series of prophecies which discuss the end times.

REVELATION

The final book of the Bible, Revelation, contains a message for the church by way of a vision received by John. From the outset of the book, we understand that the vision comes from Jesus: "The revelation from Jesus Christ, which God gave him to show his servants what must soon take place. He made it known by sending his angel to his servant John, who testifies to everything he saw—that is, the word of God and the testimony of Jesus Christ" (Rev. 1:1–2).

This vision was given to John by Jesus himself. So as we delve into this final book, it's helpful to see Revelation as an encouragement from Jesus to those in the church to continue to take the good news to the world as they look forward to his return.

But the book is also a work of prophecy. We're told in the first and last chapters that the book—or, as it is referred to, the scroll—is a prophecy. It claims to be telling of future events, or the end of days (Rev. 1:3; 22:10). Why is this important? Because this gives us a clue to what kind of lens through which we should read Revelation and understand it.

Even with this lens, however, the book of Revelation can still be difficult to read and understand. I don't want to wade into the waters of explanation right now; we don't have the space for it. But I do want to draw out a few connecting threads that link Revelation to the Bible's story.

THE ROOT OF DAVID

John is invited into the heavenly throne room, where he sees God seated on his throne. It's an incredible scene with vivid imagery, similar to what we saw in the book of Isaiah when the seraphim cried out, "Holy, holy, holy" (Isa. 6:3) as they waited on God in worship and service. Here John describes a heavenly scene in which four strange creatures repeat the same chorus day and night: "Holy, holy, holy is the Lord God Almighty, who was, and is, and is to come" (Rev. 4:8).

Then he sees an angel standing beside God's throne. The angel cries out, "Who is worthy to break the seals and open the scroll?" (Rev. 5:2). But no one is worthy to break the seals, so John begins to weep. John is comforted by one of the elders, who tells him, "Do not weep! See, the Lion of the tribe of Judah, the Root of David, has triumphed. He is able to open the scroll and its seven seals" (v. 5).

The elder in John's vision calls Jesus the Root of David. We also find Jesus referring to himself as the Root of David at the end of Revelation (Rev. 22:16). If you recall, this is a reference to the genealogy of Jesus that we discussed in chapter 10.[13] John connects Jesus with the Old Testament in this scene. But there's another connection as well.

THE SLAIN LAMB

John then sees "a Lamb, looking as if it had been slain" (Rev. 5:6) at the center of the throne. This Lamb is the one we find breaking the seals. So Jesus, who is the Root of David, is depicted as the Lamb that is breaking the seals. The chapter ends with a song in heaven.

They sang a new song, saying:

"You are worthy to take the scroll
    and to open its seals,
because you were slain,
    and with your blood you purchased for God
    persons from every tribe and language and
        people and nation.
You have made them to be a kingdom and priests to
    serve our God,
        and they will reign on the earth."

Then I looked and heard the voice of many angels, numbering thousands upon thousands, and ten thousand times ten thousand. They encircled the throne and the living creatures and the elders. In a loud voice they were saying:

"Worthy is the Lamb, who was slain,
to receive power and wealth and wisdom and
strength
and honor and glory and praise!"

Then I heard every creature in heaven and on earth and under the earth and on the sea, and all that is in them, saying:

"To him who sits on the throne and to the Lamb
be praise and honor and glory and power,
for ever and ever!"

The four living creatures said, "Amen," and the elders fell down and worshiped.

—REVELATION 5:9–14

Throughout the book of Revelation, John refers to the Lamb. This reference connects Jesus to the Passover lamb. If you recall, Philip told the Ethiopian eunuch that the text he was reading from in Isaiah 53, which said, "He was led like a lamb to the slaughter" (v. 7), was speaking of

Jesus. Now that same Lamb shows up in Revelation. And it is because of the action of this sacrificial lamb that the curse we discussed all the way back at the beginning of this book can be reversed. The Lamb, the Root of David, ushers in a new heaven and a new earth.

Here is how chapters 21 and 22 begin.

Then I saw "a new heaven and a new earth," for the first heaven and the first earth had passed away, and there was no longer any sea. I saw the Holy City, the new Jerusalem, coming down out of heaven from God, prepared as a bride beautifully dressed for her husband. And I heard a loud voice from the throne saying, "Look! God's dwelling place is now among the people, and he will dwell with them. They will be his people, and God himself will be with them and be their God. 'He will wipe every tear from their eyes. There will be no more death' or mourning or crying or pain, for the old order of things has passed away."

He who was seated on the throne said, "I am making everything new!" Then he said, "Write this down, for these words are trustworthy and true."

He said to me: "It is done. I am the Alpha and the Omega, the Beginning and the End. To the thirsty I will give water without cost from the spring of the water of life. Those who are victorious will inherit all this, and I will be their God and they will be my children. But the cowardly, the unbelieving, the vile, the murderers, the sexually immoral, those who practice magic arts, the idolaters and all liars—they will be consigned to the fiery lake of burning sulfur. This is the second death."

—REVELATION 21:1–8

Then the angel showed me the river of the water of life, as clear as crystal, flowing from the throne of God and of the Lamb down the middle of the great street of the city. On each side of the river stood the tree of life, bearing twelve crops of fruit, yielding its fruit every month. And the leaves of the tree are for the healing of the nations. No longer will there be any curse. The throne of God and of the Lamb will be in the city, and his servants will serve him. They will see his face, and his name will be on their foreheads. There will be no more night. They will not need the light of a lamp or the light of the sun, for the Lord God will give them light. And they will reign for ever and ever.

—REVELATION 22:1–5

So while there is a lot in Revelation that is debated, the book claims to be a message from Jesus and a prophecy of "what must soon take place" (Rev. 1:1). John, the author, depicts Jesus as the Root of David and as a Lamb through-out. The end of the book speaks of a new heaven and a new earth, where those who are victorious will reign for-ever and, as in the garden of Eden, there is a tree of life.

TWELVE

THE BIBLE'S CLAIMS

We've traveled from the beginning to the end to find out that the Bible tells a story—a story of a creator God who creates man for relationship with himself, but man's disobedience breaks that relationship. And God the Redeemer, out of love, provides the way of restoration. It's a beautiful story.

But there's more to the story. There's something different about the Bible. The Bible makes some very bold claims. Let's take a look at a few.

CLAIM 1: THERE IS A GOD, AND
THE BIBLE IS HIS WORD

The biggest and boldest claim of the Bible is that there is a God and that the Bible is his Word. From the very outset, the Bible assumes there is a God, when it starts with, "In the beginning God . . ." (Gen. 1:1). It claims to be telling the story of God.

The Bible repeatedly refers to itself as the Word of God. The phrases "word of God," "words of God," "word of the Lord," or "commandments of the Lord" appear more than 350 times in the King James Version of the Bible. Over and over, the Bible is claiming to be God's Word.

When Moses gave the Ten Commandments to the people of Israel at Mount Sinai, he said simply, "God spoke all these words, saying . . ." (Ex. 20:1 ESV). As the story goes, God called Moses up to the top of the mountain and gave him instructions for the people to live by. God also wrote down his law on tablets of stone. We know these rules as the Ten Commandments. Moses went back down the mountain to give God's law to the people.

We are told Moses was a messenger of God. He was bringing God's message of the law to the people. The law represented a code of conduct—a way of living. If the people obeyed the law of God, then their obedience would keep them in harmony with God.

Similarly, in the book of Matthew, Jesus referred to the law of Moses as from God. Responding to a question from the Pharisees and scribes, his detractors, Jesus said, "Why do you break the command of God for the sake of your tradition? For God said, 'Honor your father and mother' and 'Anyone who curses their father or mother is to be put to death.' But you say that if anyone declares that what might have been used to help their father or mother is 'devoted to God,' they are not to 'honor their father or mother' with it. Thus you nullify the word of God for the sake of your tradition" (Matt. 15:3–6).

The Word of God was considered so sacred that the Israelites were instructed to never add to it nor take from it. In Deuteronomy 4:2, Moses told them, "You shall not add to the word that I command you, or take from it, that you may keep the commandments of the LORD your God that I command you" (ESV).

CLAIM 2: THE BIBLE IS INSPIRED BY GOD

While the Bible claims to be the Word of God, it also makes the claim that God was very important in its writing, that he inspired the writers as they wrote.

Peter, the disciple of Jesus, says it simply: "Above all, you must understand that no prophecy of Scripture came about by the prophet's own interpretation of things. For prophecy never had its origin in the human will, but prophets, though human, spoke from God as they were carried along by the Holy Spirit" (2 Peter 1:20–21).

In essence, Peter is saying that God's Word doesn't come from the will of men; it comes from men inspired by the Holy Spirit.

It is after his Damascus Road experience with Jesus that Paul becomes a prolific writer of letters to the various churches scattered throughout the New Testament world. Like Peter, he says it plainly: "All Scripture is God-breathed" (2 Tim. 3:16).

In his letter to the church in Corinth, Paul explains that mankind, being finite and limited, cannot grasp or imagine the infinite nature of God. So man must depend on inspiration from the Spirit of God.

However, as it is written:

"What no eye has seen,
     what no ear has heard,
and what no human mind has conceived"—
     the things God has prepared for those who
          love him—

these are the things God has revealed to us by
his Spirit.
     The Spirit searches all things, even the deep things
of God.

—1 CORINTHIANS 2:9–10

CLAIM 3: THE BIBLE IS ALIVE AND JUDGES THE HEART

In addition to claiming to be inspired, the Bible claims to be living. Hebrews 4:12 says, "The word of God is alive and active. Sharper than any double-edged sword, it penetrates even to dividing soul and spirit, joints and marrow; it judges the thoughts and attitudes of the heart."

Living? Active? Penetrating? Able to judge the thoughts and attitudes of the heart? It's a book—ink and paper—yet it claims to be alive. Strong claims. Strong words.

CLAIM 4: THE BIBLE IS RELEVANT—A SOURCE OF INSTRUCTION

One of the consistent themes throughout the Bible is its insistence that it is instructive and relevant for living. Moses, the lawgiver, said it strongly when he told the Israelites that the Word of God was their very life. "He said to them, 'Take to heart all the words I have solemnly declared to you this day, so that you may command your children to obey carefully all the words of this law. They are not just idle words for you—they are your life. By them you will live long in the land you are crossing the Jordan to possess'" (Deut. 32:46–47).

Remember Joshua, the person who succeeded Moses as the leader of Israel? The Bible records that God instructed

Joshua to "be careful to obey all the law my servant Moses gave you; do not turn from it to the right or to the left, that you may be successful" (Josh. 1:7). Further, God told Joshua to "meditate on it day and night" (v. 8) and promised that if he did so, "then you will be prosperous and successful" (v. 8).

The longest chapter in the Bible, Psalm 119, testifies to the effectiveness and sufficiency of the Bible. Every verse references God's instruction. The first eight verses use six different synonyms for God's instruction: law, statutes, ways, precepts, decrees, and commands.

> Blessed are those whose ways are blameless,
>   who walk according to the law of the LORD.
> Blessed are those who keep his statutes
>   and seek him with all their heart—
> they do no wrong
>   but follow his ways.
> You have laid down precepts
>   that are to be fully obeyed.
> Oh, that my ways were steadfast
>   in obeying your decrees!
> Then I would not be put to shame
>   when I consider all your commands.
> I will praise you with an upright heart
>   as I learn your righteous laws.
> I will obey your decrees;
>   do not utterly forsake me.
>
> —PSALM 119:1–8

In just the first 8 verses, the writer claims he will not be put to shame but his ways will be blessed as a result of keeping the Lord's Word. This continues for all 176 verses of this chapter.

Back one hundred chapters, in Psalm 19, King David wrote of God's Word,

> The law of the LORD is perfect,
> refreshing the soul.
> The statutes of the LORD are trustworthy,
> making wise the simple.
>
> —PSALM 19:7

And 2 Timothy 3:16 sums it up when it says that the Bible "is useful for teaching, rebuking, correcting and training in righteousness."

CLAIM 5: THE BIBLE WILL LAST FOREVER

As if it's not enough for the Bible to claim that it's God's Word, that it's inspired, living, active, and relevant, it also claims that it will last forever. Now, that's a long time!

King David acknowledges this in Psalm 119:89: "Your word, LORD, is eternal; it stands firm in the heavens." Later, David repeats the thought in Psalm 119:152: "Long ago I learned from your statutes that you established them to last forever."

Isaiah echoes the same thought: "The grass withers and the flowers fall, but the word of our God endures forever" (Isa. 40:8). And to make it clear, the theme continues in the New Testament, where Jesus says, "Heaven and earth will pass away, but my words will never pass away" (Matt. 24:35). In 1 Peter 1:25, the Bible says, "The word of the Lord endures forever."

Do you know what I find incredible? This book that makes such a bold claim happens to be the one that has more manuscript evidence than any major classical work. There are between six hundred and seven hundred known copies of Homer's *Iliad*, while there are more than five thousand manuscripts of the New Testament in existence. Interesting.

THE BIBLE'S SIGNIFICANCE

With such bold claims, how could anybody take the Bible seriously? Yet many have. While there are differences in culture, economic status, education, and political and social situations, the Bible is the best-selling book around the world. That status has remained unchanged. Daniel Radosh, writing for the *New Yorker*, says it this way: "The familiar observation that the Bible is the best-selling book of all time obscures a more startling fact: the Bible is the best-selling book of the year, every year."[14]

The writer John Dickson entertains the question of why the Bible continues to outsell all other books. Skeptics, he says, might say, "Well, that's because the church imposes it on the world." That might be some of it, Dickson admits. But he believes the reason is because the Bible "tells a story that people long to be true."[15]

Throughout the years, the Bible has continued to have an impact on individual lives and in the world. In the year 2000, *Life* magazine came out with a publication titled *The Life Millennium: The 100 Most Important Events and People of the Past 1,000 Years*. It was of course a subjective listing, but they endeavored to come up with a list. Here are the top ten.

10. The Compass Goes to Sea
9. Hitler Comes to Power
8. The Declaration of Independence
7. Gunpowder Weapons
6. Germ Theory
5. Galileo's Telescope
4. The Industrial Revolution
3. Luther Knocks
2. Columbus's Voyage

This list includes both the good and the bad; Hitler coming to power, I think we can agree, was not a good thing. So I think it would be better to call the events the most impactful rather than the most important, as I find it hard to say that the Holocaust was important, but it did impact the world.

But what was the number one item on the list?

Gutenberg prints the Bible!

Notice that it wasn't the Gutenberg press; it was Gutenberg prints the Bible. I don't believe any of us fully understand the degree to which the printing of the Bible has influenced our world. A quick Google search will reveal the many books people have written over the years about the Bible and its impact, but it still remains difficult to fully comprehend the ripple effect of that event. Scientists, writers, builders, composers, presidents, kings and queens, peasants, and the lame have all been influenced by this book.

Because of the significance of the Bible, it would seem important for a person to possess a basic understanding of it. I am not alone in that assessment. The well-known atheist Richard Dawkins, an Oxford-trained evolutionary biologist, wrote a book called *The God Delusion*. In it, he argues that the King James Version of the Bible should be taught for "literary culture." After he makes the argument, he gives more than one hundred examples of phrases from our language that come from the King James Version of the Bible, such as "an eye for an eye," "the writing on the wall," and "the good Samaritan."

How many times have you heard a news story of someone acting as a good Samaritan? If you don't know the good Samaritan story, you are to a degree illiterate in our society. Though Dawkins is not making a case for believing in the God of the Bible, even he admits that studying the Bible—at the very least, as literature—possesses some merit.

It has been said that you can't understand Shakespeare if you don't know the Bible. Why? Because Shakespeare knew his King James Bible and used many references to the Bible in his writings. The same could be said of much in our society, from political speeches to movies to music to literature.

It seems to me, we do a disservice to students by not teaching the basic facts of the Bible, especially in a country in which so many of the principles the founders employed to establish our government stem from the Bible. The idea that all men are created equal is a biblical concept and helped inform the thinking of the American founders.

RIGHT READING

I do hope, now that you understand the story line and know some of the Bible's bold claims and incredible impact, that you will be inspired to go deeper and read the whole story for yourself, in the same way that I went back and watched *Les Misérables*. If at some point you get stuck, just remember: nobody has it all figured out; you're not alone.

The Bible has some good advice here as well. It tells us

it has to be correctly handled. That is what Paul is advising Timothy in his second letter to him. He says, "Do your best to present yourself to God as one approved, a worker who does not need to be ashamed and who correctly handles the word of truth" (2 Tim. 2:15). Paul is telling Timothy he has to correctly understand the Scriptures.

Elsewhere in the New Testament, we find Luke commending a group of Jews because they were examining the Scriptures daily to see if what Paul and Silas were teaching was correct. "Now the Berean Jews were of more noble character than those in Thessalonica, for they received the message with great eagerness and examined the Scriptures every day to see if what Paul said was true" (Acts 17:11).

Unfortunately, there are those who do not respond to the Bible like the Bereans did. There always have been, and there always will be, those out there who will use the Bible for their own selfish intent, and those who will misrepresent what the Bible teaches. But you can take on this noble pursuit: examine the Scriptures; find out for yourself what the Bible says.

CONCLUSION

This brings us to the question of whether the Bible is true. I mentioned in the introduction that there are millions who believe the Bible is true, and millions who don't. To believe the Bible, you have to believe its first claim, that there is a God, which is a matter of faith.

Today when you buy a book, it falls into a category. Is it fiction or nonfiction? A fictional story is often labeled a novel. It says it right on the front of the book, and you know it when you buy it. The Bible never claims to be a novel. On the contrary, it is written as if it is recording actual historical events. The Bible claims it is true, that there really is a God who created the world.

If it is not true, it creates many interesting questions. Who did write this book? How could so many people be fooled into believing it is what it claims to be? How could something made up have such an impact on governments, science, education, literature, music, and art? Think of all the energy, time, and money spent on building churches and synagogues, on writing books and studying in universities. All that time spent on this one book.

Millions of people credit the Bible for changing their lives. They were hopeless but then found hope when they heard the Bible's story. People on every continent, from different cultures, speaking different languages, from the wealthy to those with little means, from the most educated to the least—all have been impacted by this book.

You will ultimately decide what you believe about the Bible. I invite you to investigate it for yourself with an open mind. If you, like some, refuse to consider that there could be an all-powerful God who can do the supernatural, then you have already determined your conclusion. Would that be open-minded? Why not explore the evidence for yourself?

C. S. Lewis was an atheist. But he explored the Bible for himself, through reading it and through conversations with his friends. Lewis writes, "Christianity, if false, is of no importance, and if true, of infinite importance. The only thing it cannot be is moderately important."

In the first eleven chapters of this book, I tried to tell the Bible's story without assuming it is true. I wanted the Bible, as much as possible, to speak for itself. I wanted to look at the Bible, starting from scratch—to simply know its story. If the story is true and the biblical timeline is accurate, that means it took more than forty writers over fifteen hundred years to write it. That alone would make this book unlike anything ever written.

Adding to that, those writers were writing in three different languages, on three different continents, from all different walks of life. Some were writing from the depths of despair; others, from the heights of joy; still others, from prison or from a throne. They were fishermen, peasants, cupbearers, and kings. And if all that isn't enough, the most incredible aspect is that they were all writing one unified story.

A story that has a beginning, a problem, a resolution, and an end. It's a story that foretells of events—events that would happen hundreds of years in the future. If the story is true, then some of those predictions have been fulfilled, and some of them are yet to be fulfilled.

And amazingly, if this story *is* true, you and I find ourselves right in the middle of it!

I believe the story is true, but you shouldn't take my word for it. Read it and investigate it for yourself, and see if I've got it right. Let the Bible speak for itself. My hope is that you will, if you haven't already, come to believe and love this beautiful story told by this beautiful book!

APPENDIX

COMPLETE LIST OF THE BOOKS OF THE BIBLE

OLD TESTAMENT

Genesis
Exodus
Leviticus
Numbers
Deuteronomy
Joshua
Judges
Ruth
1 Samuel
2 Samuel

1 Kings

2 Kings

1 Chronicles

2 Chronicles

Ezra

Nehemiah

Esther

Job

Psalms

Proverbs

Ecclesiastes

Song of Songs

Isaiah

Jeremiah

Lamentations

Ezekiel

Daniel

Hosea

Joel

Amos

Obadiah

Jonah

Micah

Nahum

Habakkuk

Zephaniah

Haggai

Zechariah

Malachi

NEW TESTAMENT

Matthew

Mark

Luke

John

Acts

Romans

1 Corinthians

2 Corinthians

Galatians

Ephesians

Philippians

Colossians

1 Thessalonians

2 Thessalonians

1 Timothy

2 Timothy

Titus

Philemon

Hebrews

James

1 Peter

2 Peter

1 John

2 John

3 John

Jude

Revelation

NOTES

1. Pew Research Center, "Religion in the Public Schools," May 9, 2007, *www.pewforum.org/2007/05/09/religion -in-the-public-schools/* (January 18, 2019).
2. Bonnie Blackburn and Leofranc Holford-Strevens, *The Oxford Companion to the Year: An Exploration of Calendar Customs and Time-Reckoning*, 1st ed. (Oxford; New York: Oxford Univ. Press, 1999), 782.
3. "The land enjoyed its sabbath rests; all the time of its desolation it rested, until the seventy years were completed in fulfillment of the word of the LORD spoken by Jeremiah" (2 Chron. 36:21). "In the first year of [Darius's] reign, I, Daniel, understood from the Scriptures, according to the word of the LORD given to Jeremiah the prophet, that the desolation of Jerusalem would last seventy years" (Dan. 9:2).
4. "This is what the LORD says: 'When seventy years are completed for Babylon, I will come to you and fulfill my good promise to bring you back to this place'" (Jer. 29:10).
5. Biblica, "Intro to Judges," October 7, 2016, *www.biblica*

.com/resources/scholar-notes/niv-study-bible/intro-to
-judges/ (January 3, 2019).

6. "The Lord will scatter you among the peoples, and only a few of you will survive among the nations to which the Lord will drive you. There you will worship man-made gods of wood and stone, which cannot see or hear or eat or smell" (Deut. 4:27–28).

7. For more verses on the foretold captivity of Israel, see 2 Kings 20:17; 21:10–15; 24:2, 10–16; Jeremiah 34:2.

8. Bible Study Tools, "A Guide to the Ten Commandments," March 28, 2017, www.biblestudytools.com/bible-stories /the-10-commandments-bible-verse-list-and-meaning. html (February 7, 2019).

9. Jonathan Petersen, "The 10 Most Popular Books of the Bible," *Bible Gateway Blog*, April 21, 2014, www .biblegateway.com/blog/2014/04/the-10-most-popular -books-of-the-bible-and-why/ (March 27, 2019).

10. Alan Cole, *Mark*, New Bible Commentary: 21st Century Edition, ed. D. A. Carson et al., Accordance electronic ed. (Downers Grove: InterVarsity Press, 1994), 946, *https:// accordance.bible/link/read/IVP-NB_Commentary#12507.*

11. Donald Guthrie, *John*, New Bible Commentary: 21st Century Edition, ed. D. A. Carson et al., Accordance electronic ed. (Downers Grove: InterVarsity Press, 1994), 1022, *https://accordance.bible/link/read/IVP-NB _Commentary#13380.*

12. For more on how Jesus fulfilled the Old Testament law, see Hebrews 9:12; 7:23–24; John 4:21, 23.

13. See these other references for where Jesus is referred to as the Root of Jesse (David's father): Isaiah 11:10; Romans 15:12.

14. Daniel Radosh, "The Good Book Business: Why Publishers Love the Bible," *New Yorker* (December 18, 2006).

15. Jeremy Bouma, "Why Is the Bible Always the Number One Bestseller?" April 22, 2015, *https:// zondervanacademic.com/blog/why-is-the-bible-always -the-number-one-bestseller/* (April 2, 2019).